Coloring Harmony

A Collection of Coloring Pages and Inspirational Haiku Poems

Quiet woodland path,

Nature's whispers soothe the soul,

Peace blooms with each step.

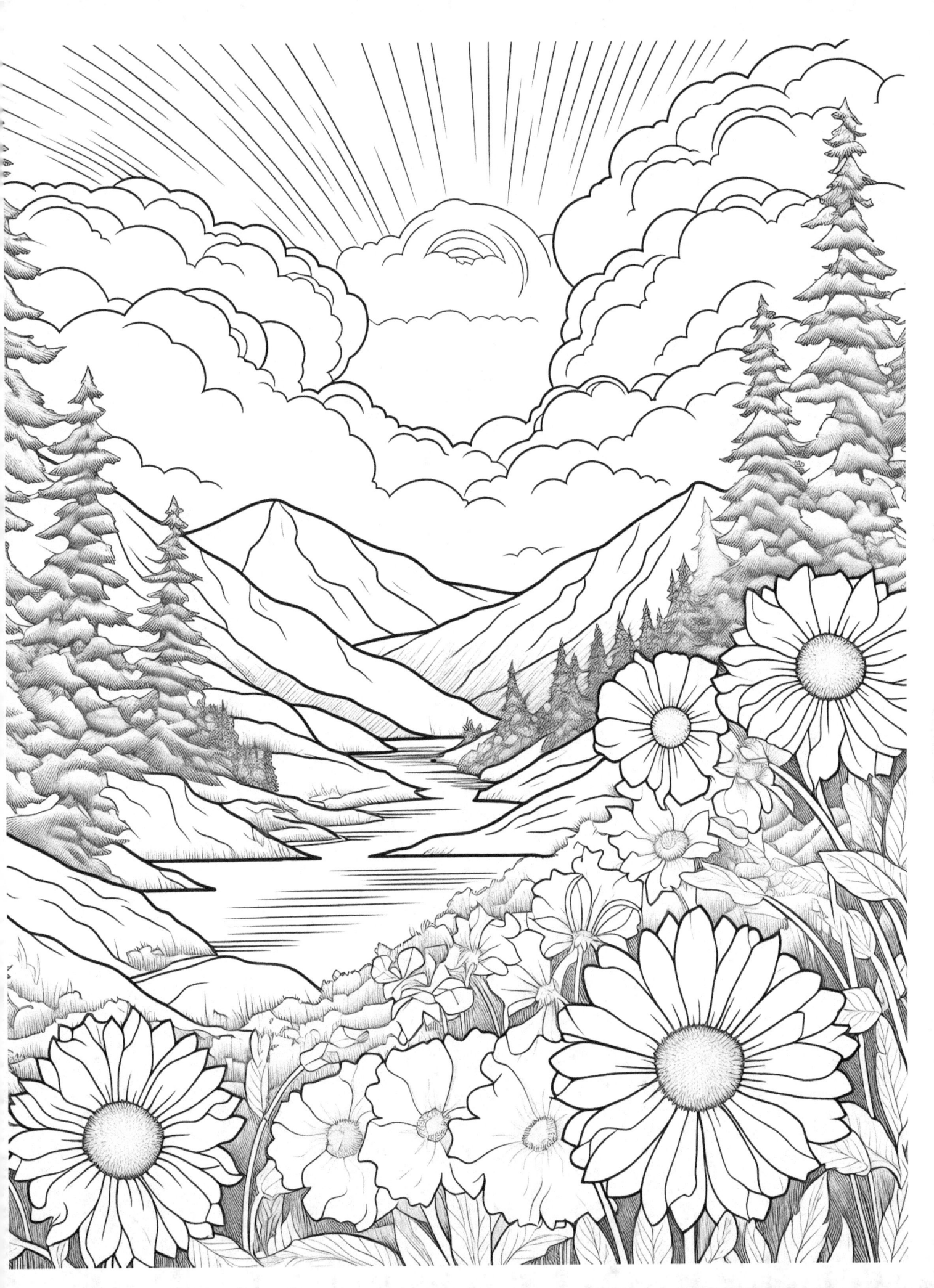

Embrace ebb and flow,

Acceptance, a gentle stream,

Heart finds calm repose.

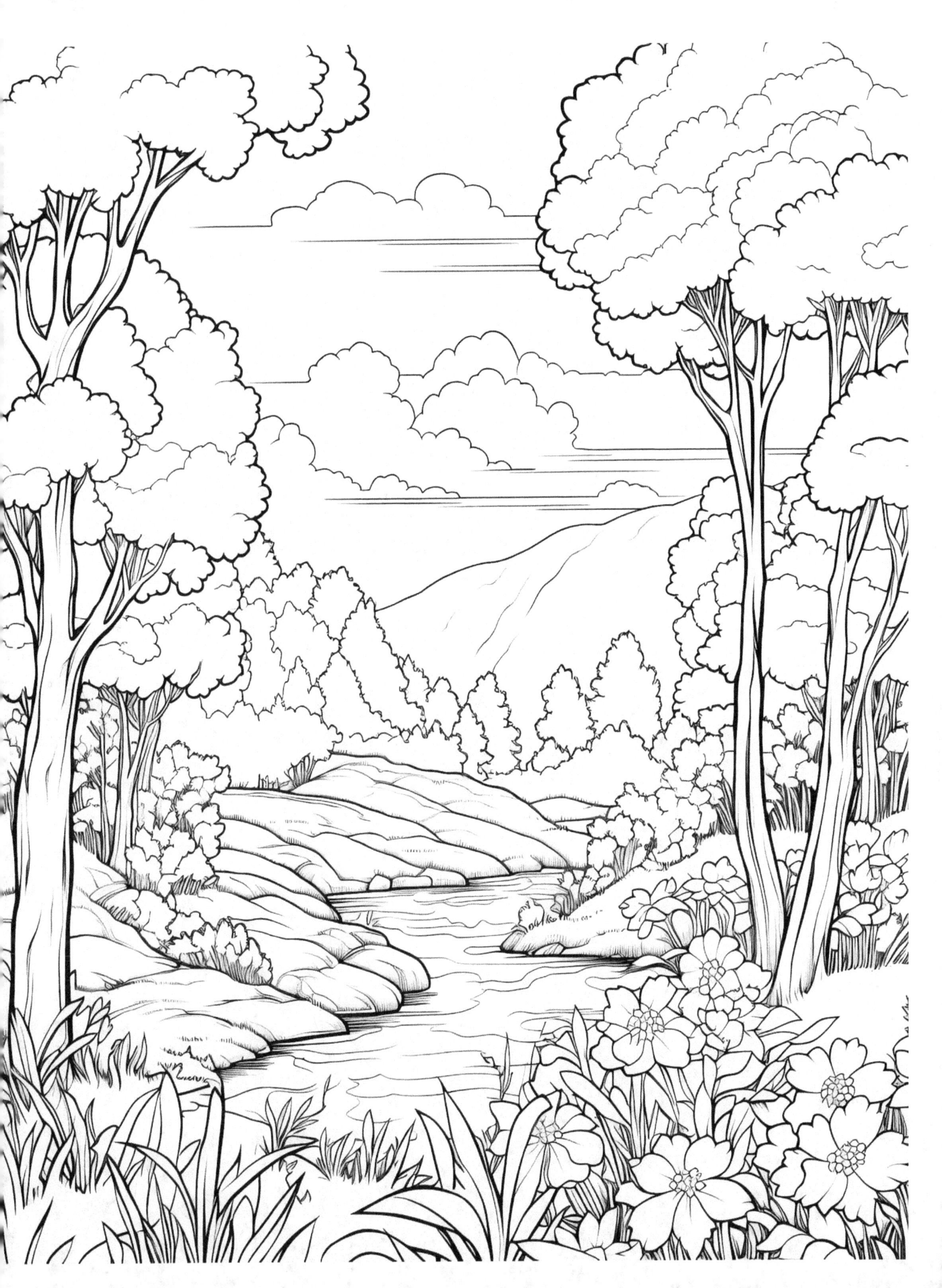

Ancient stones still stand,

Weathered by time's gentle touch,

Time's testament strong.

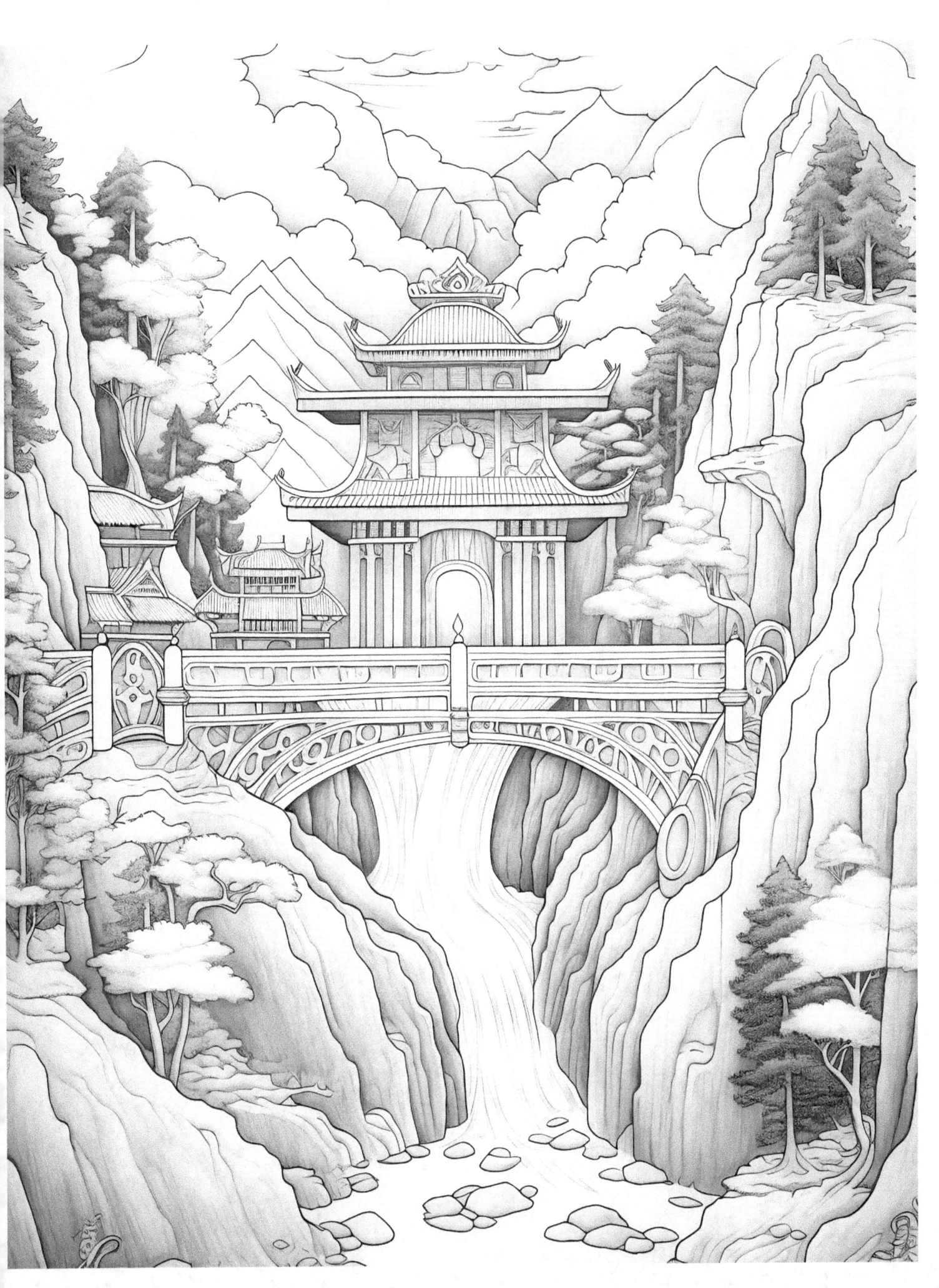

Silent strength within,

Roots of resilience endure,

Whispers speak power.

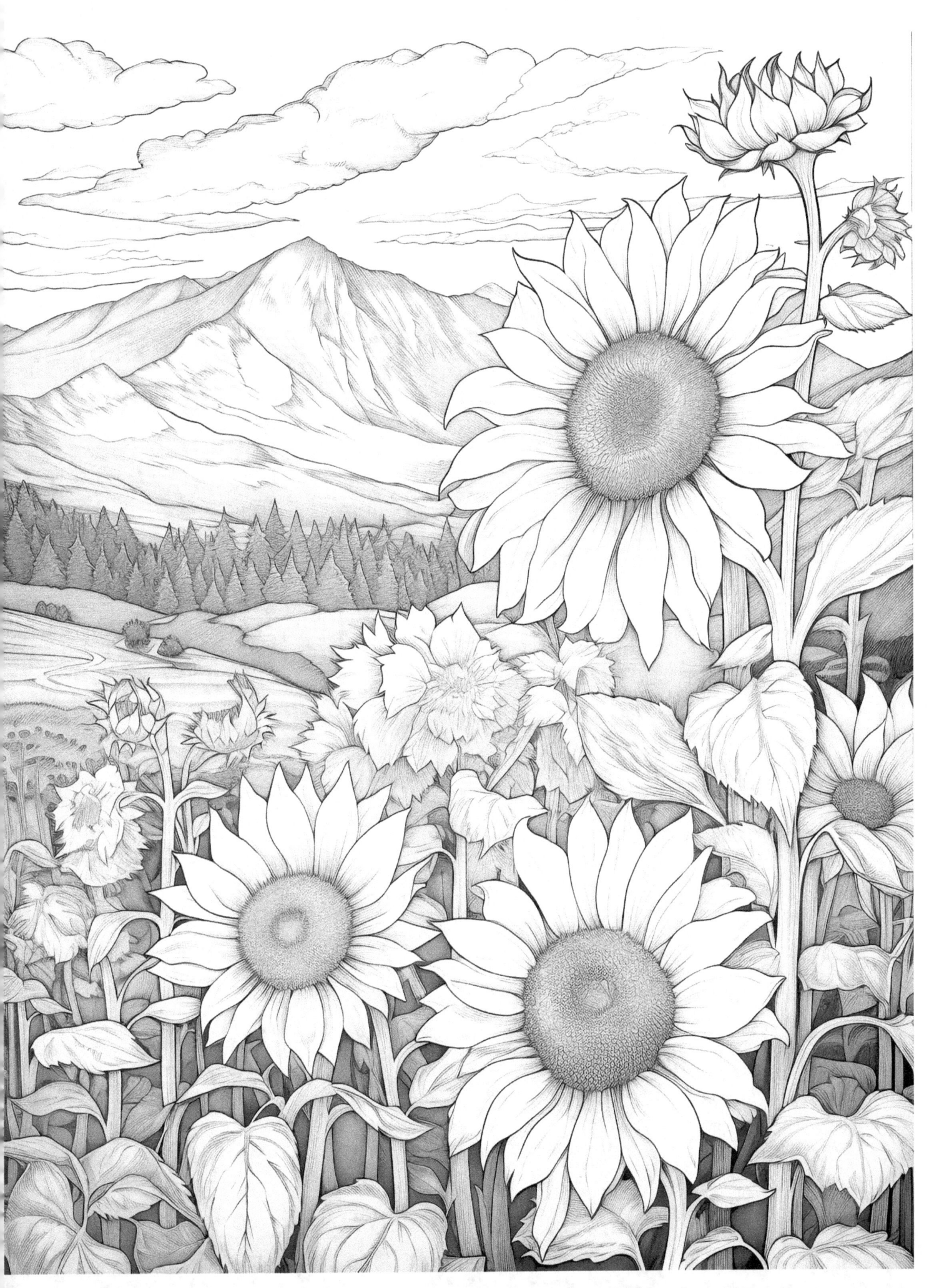

Moonlight on still pond,

Silent reflections ripple,

Thoughts echo softly.

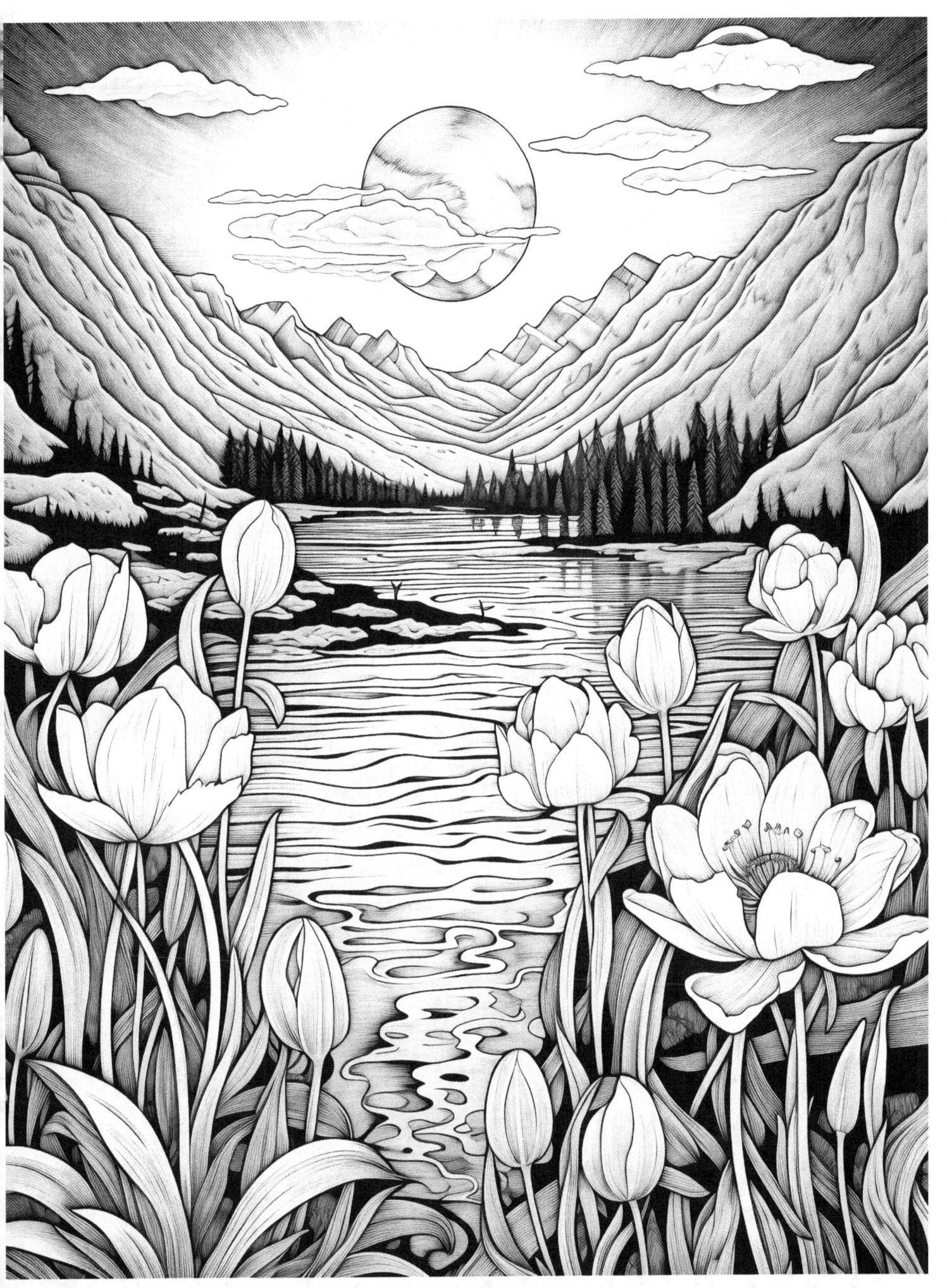

Neatly aligned paths,

Order in chaos finds peace,

Structured harmony.

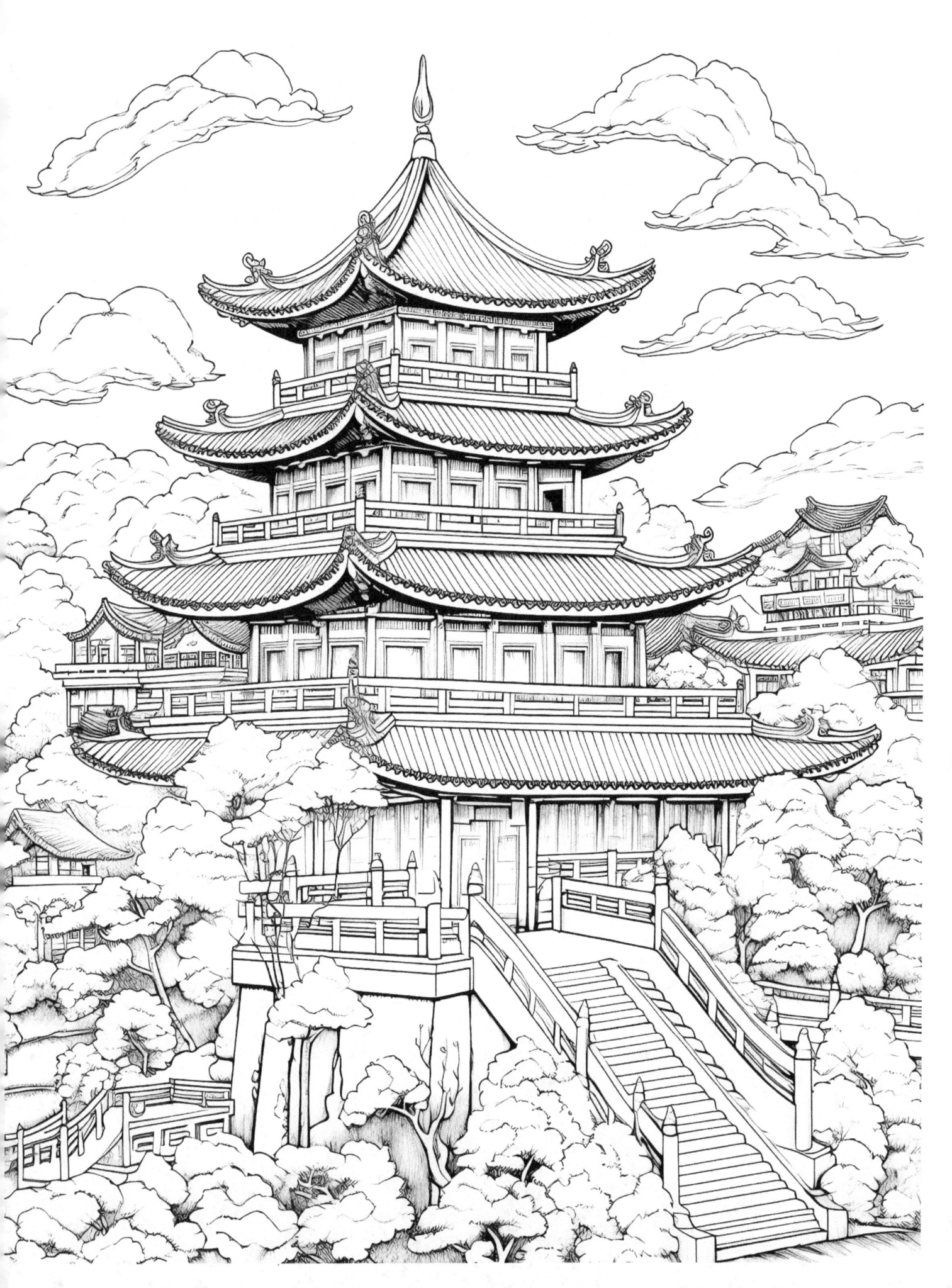

Mountains touch the sky,

Perspective shapes horizons,

Mind's lens, truth unfolds.

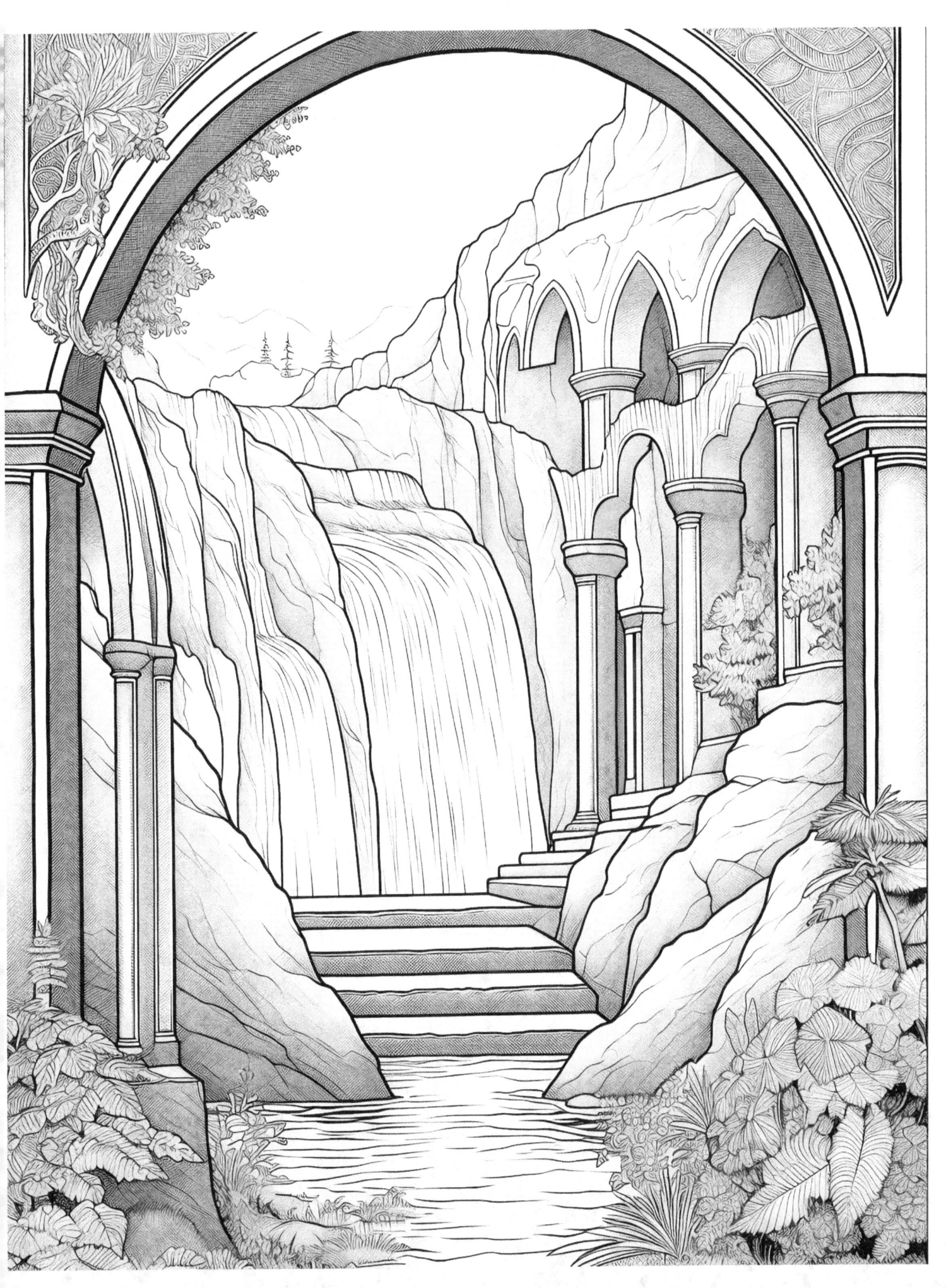

Sunset's warm embrace,

Simple joys in fleeting time,

Gratitude blossoms.

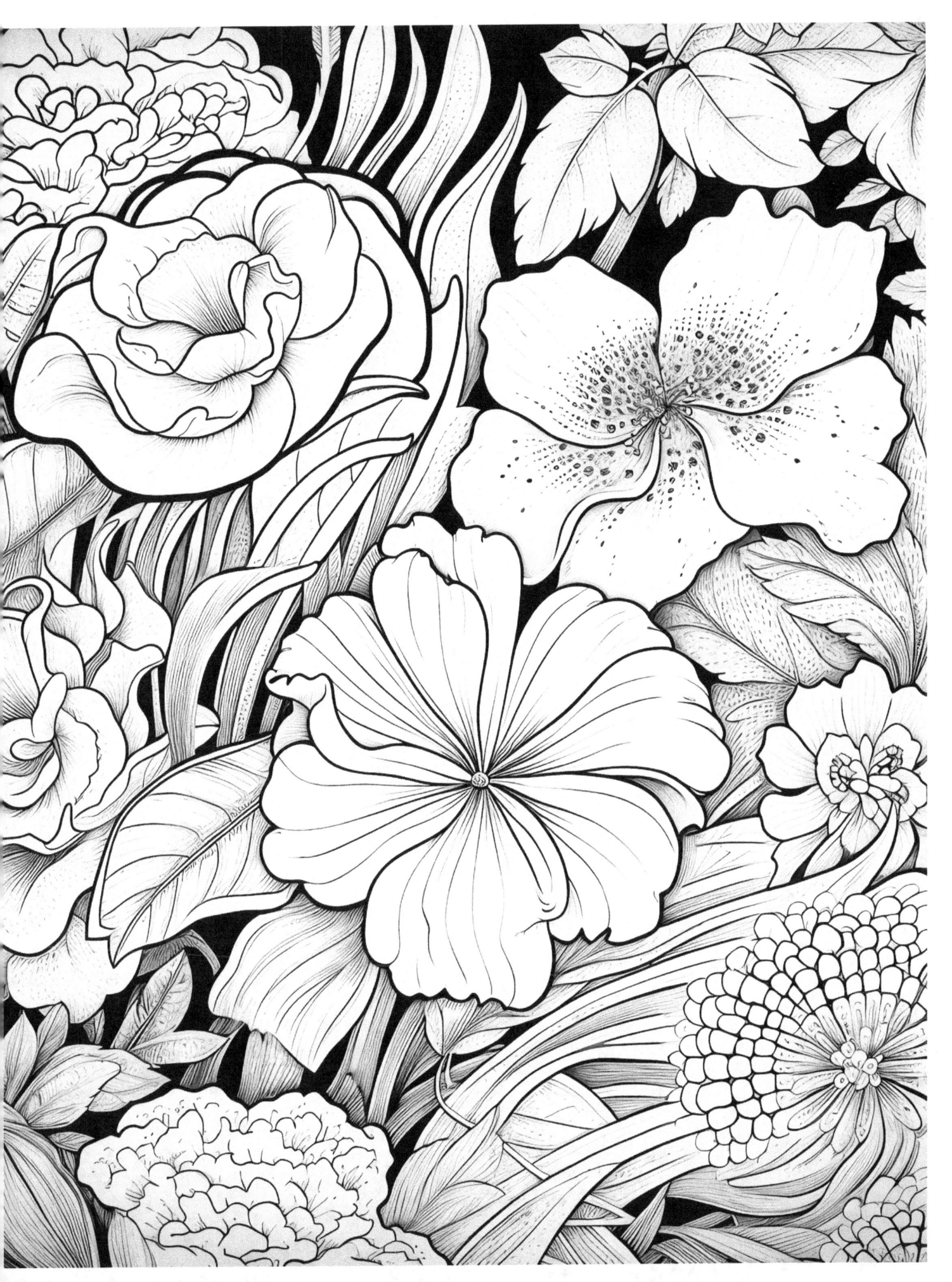

Starlight leads the way,

Guiding light in darkened skies,

Hope's beacon persists.

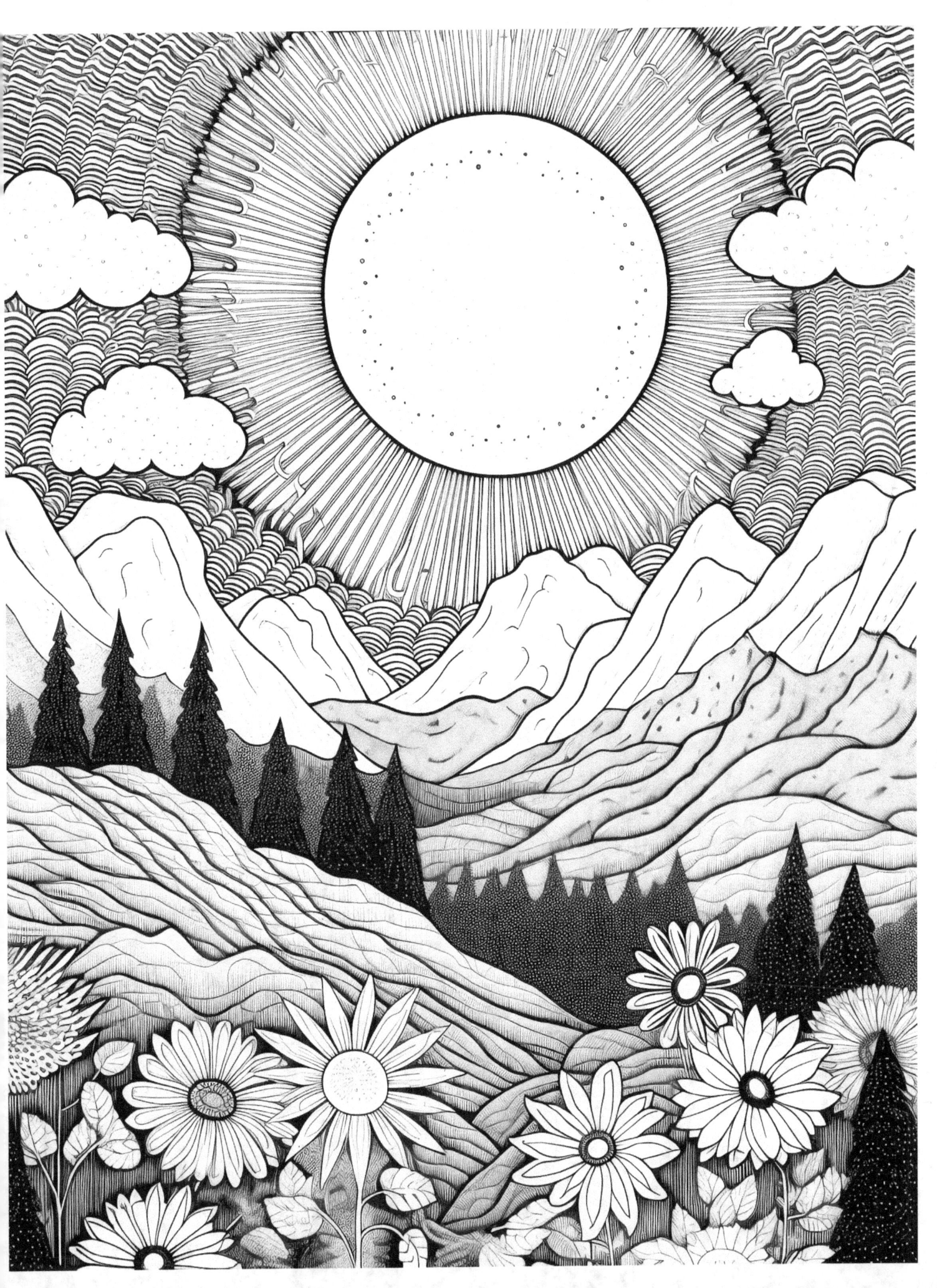

Tranquil waters flow,

Whispers of peace in the breeze,

Calm cradles the soul.

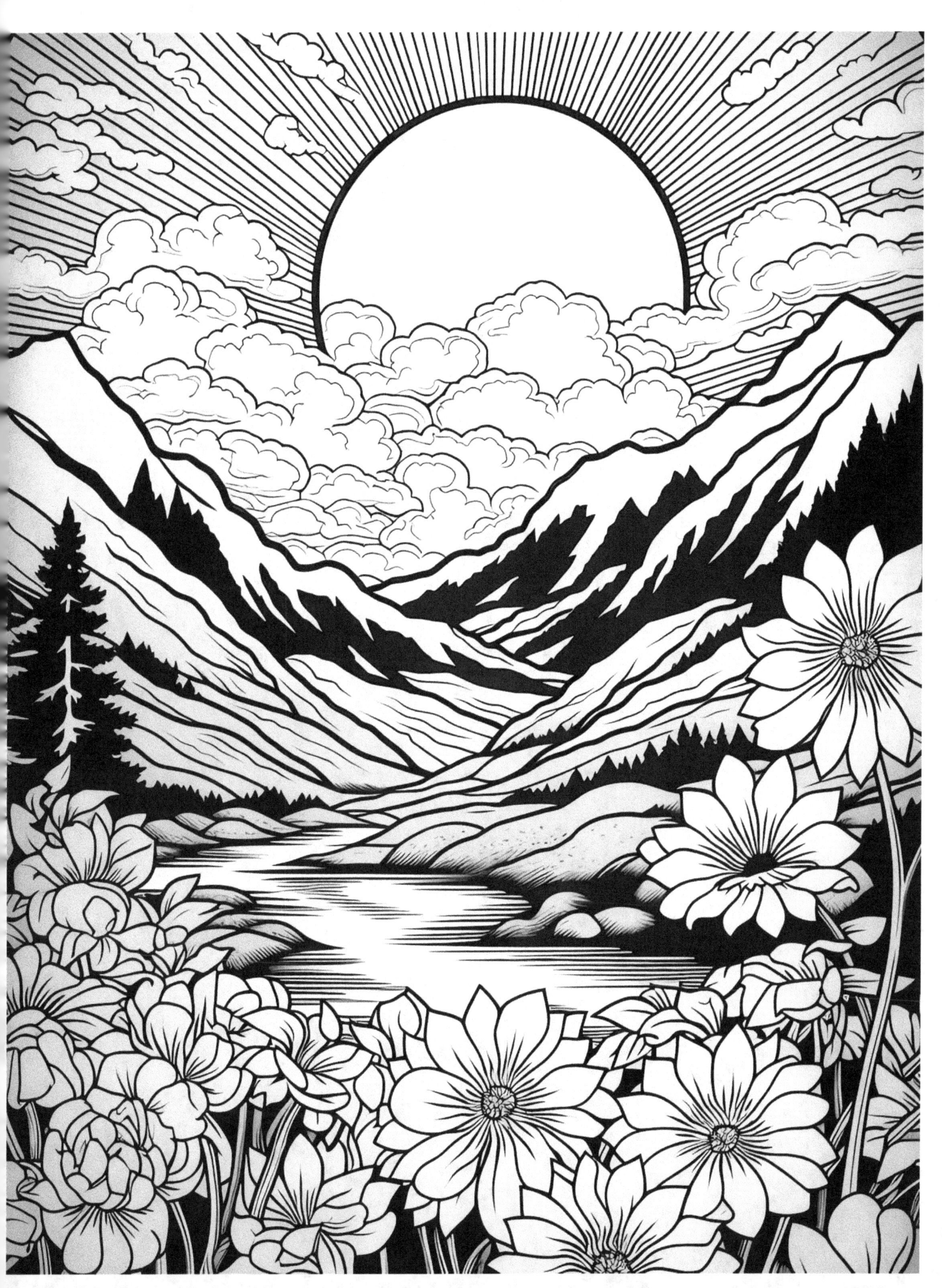

Nature's dance unfolds,

Balance teeters, finds its grace,

Harmony in flow.

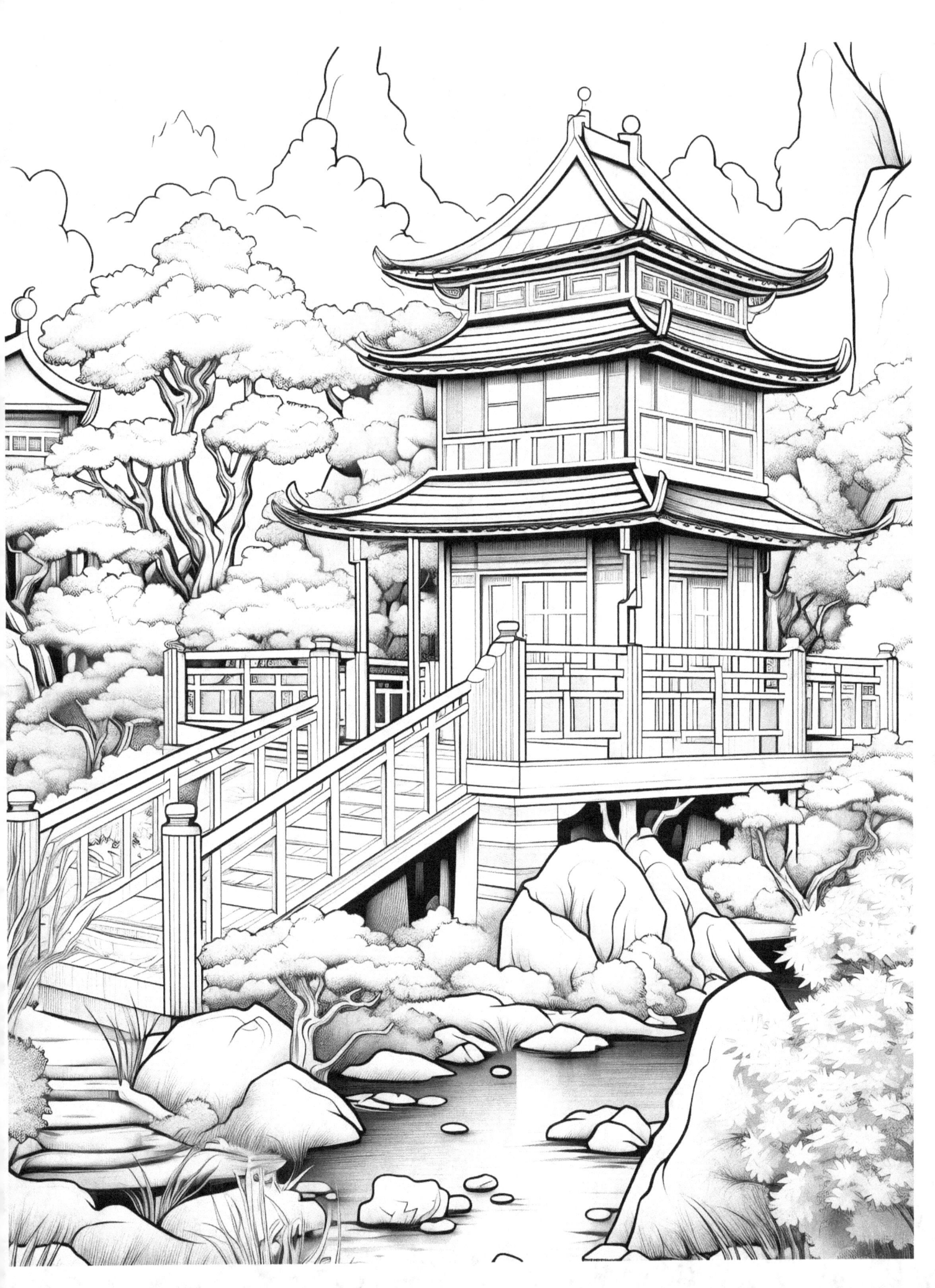

Silent words of care,

Respect blooms in gentle deeds,

Heartfelt echoes speak.

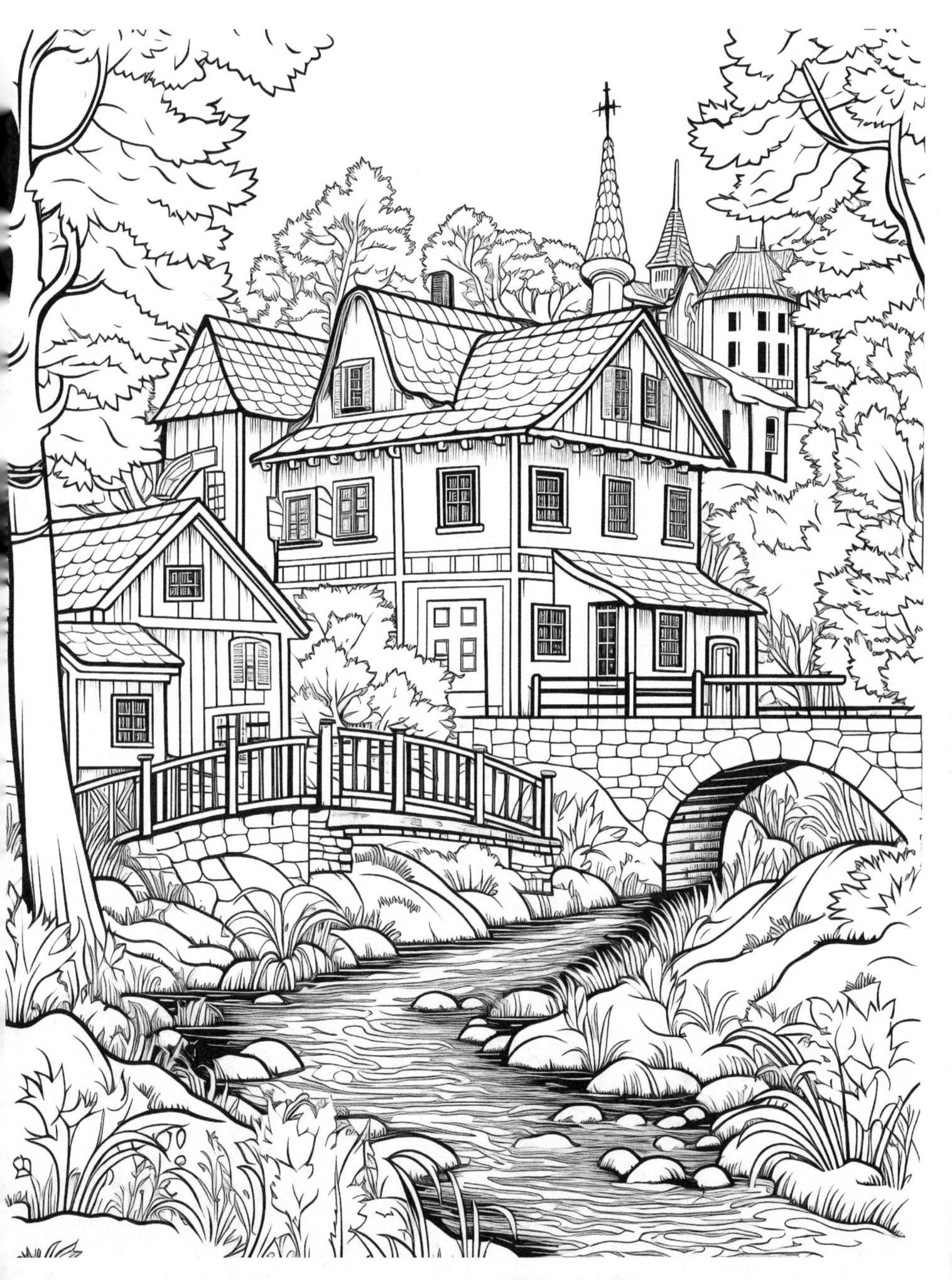

Shadows weave their tales,

Resilient spirit ignites,

Dawn within the dark.

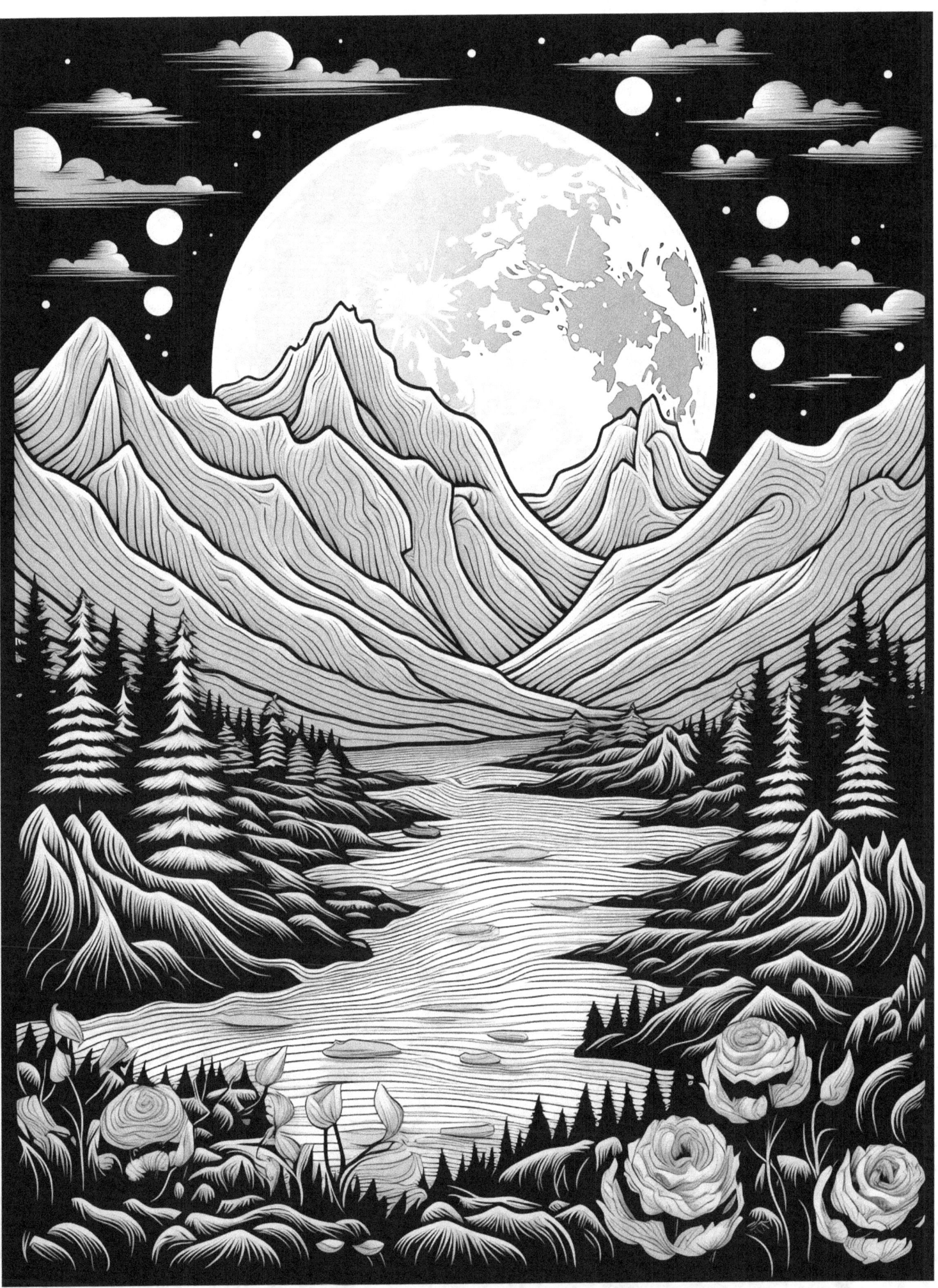

Desert winds may sting,

Resilience in arid trials,

Survival's pure song.

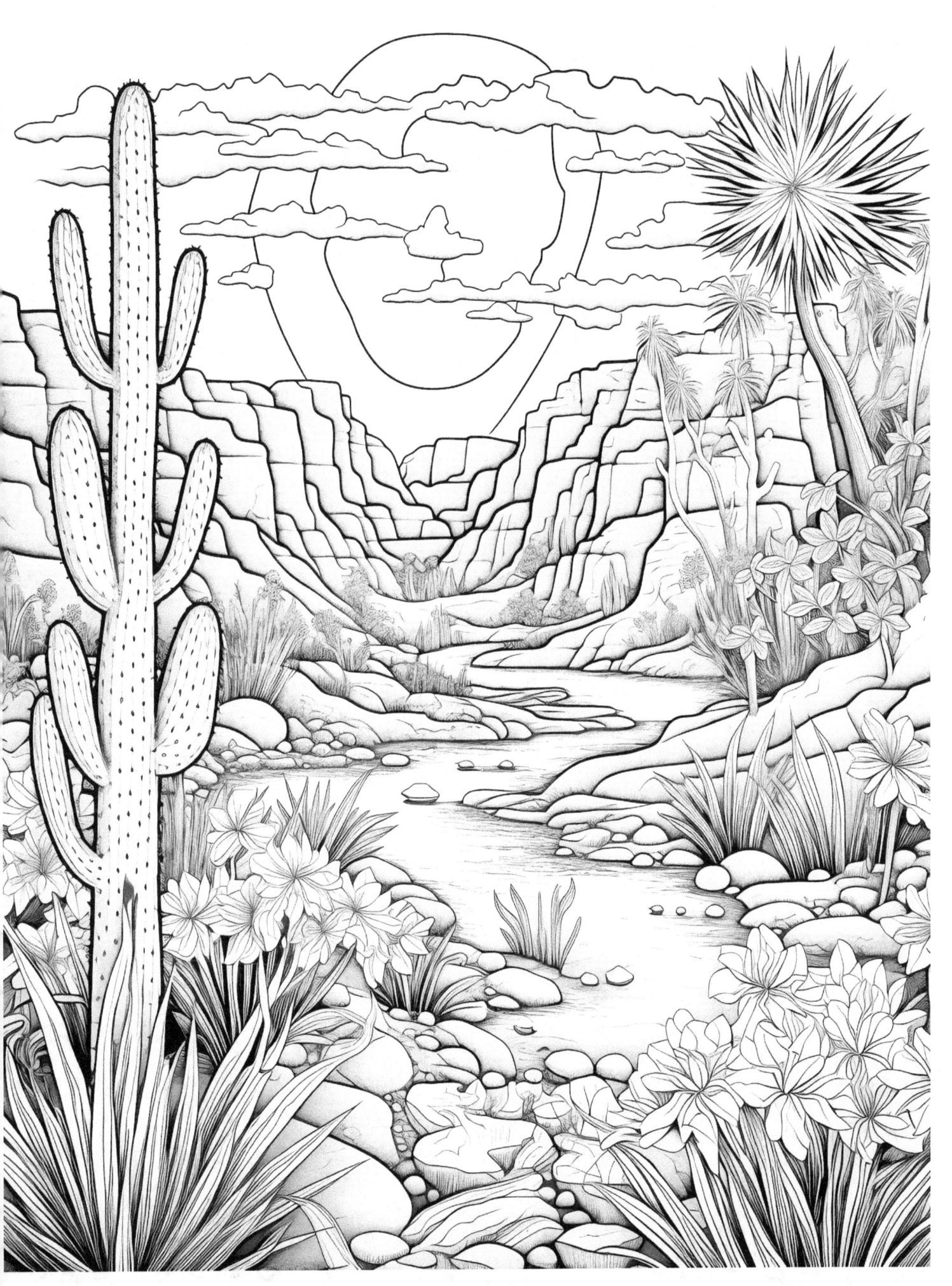

Roots in rocky soil,

Thriving amidst life's fierce storms,

Strength blooms in the rough.

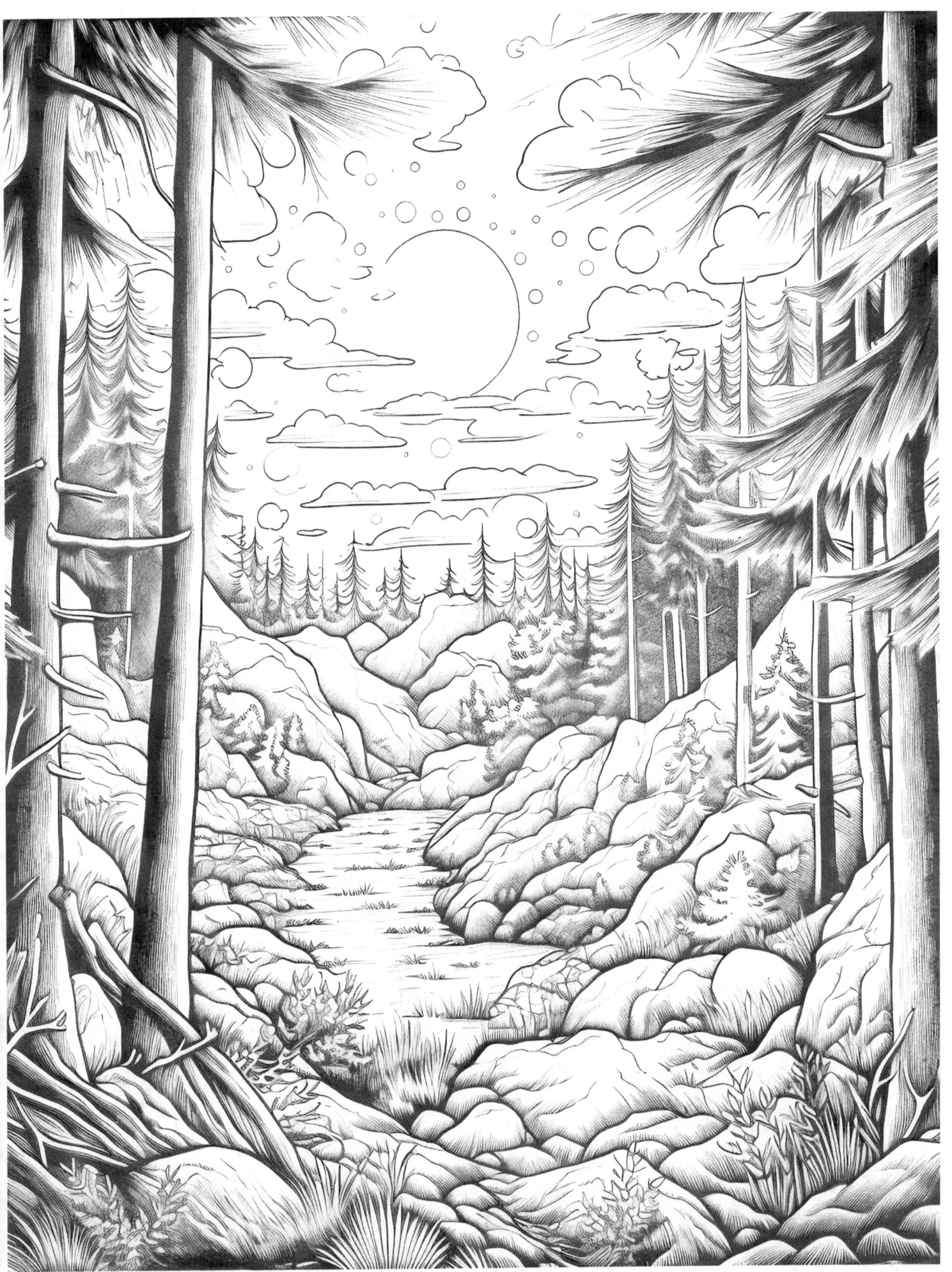

Eyes fixed on the prize,

Goals shine on determined gaze,

Focused steps forward.

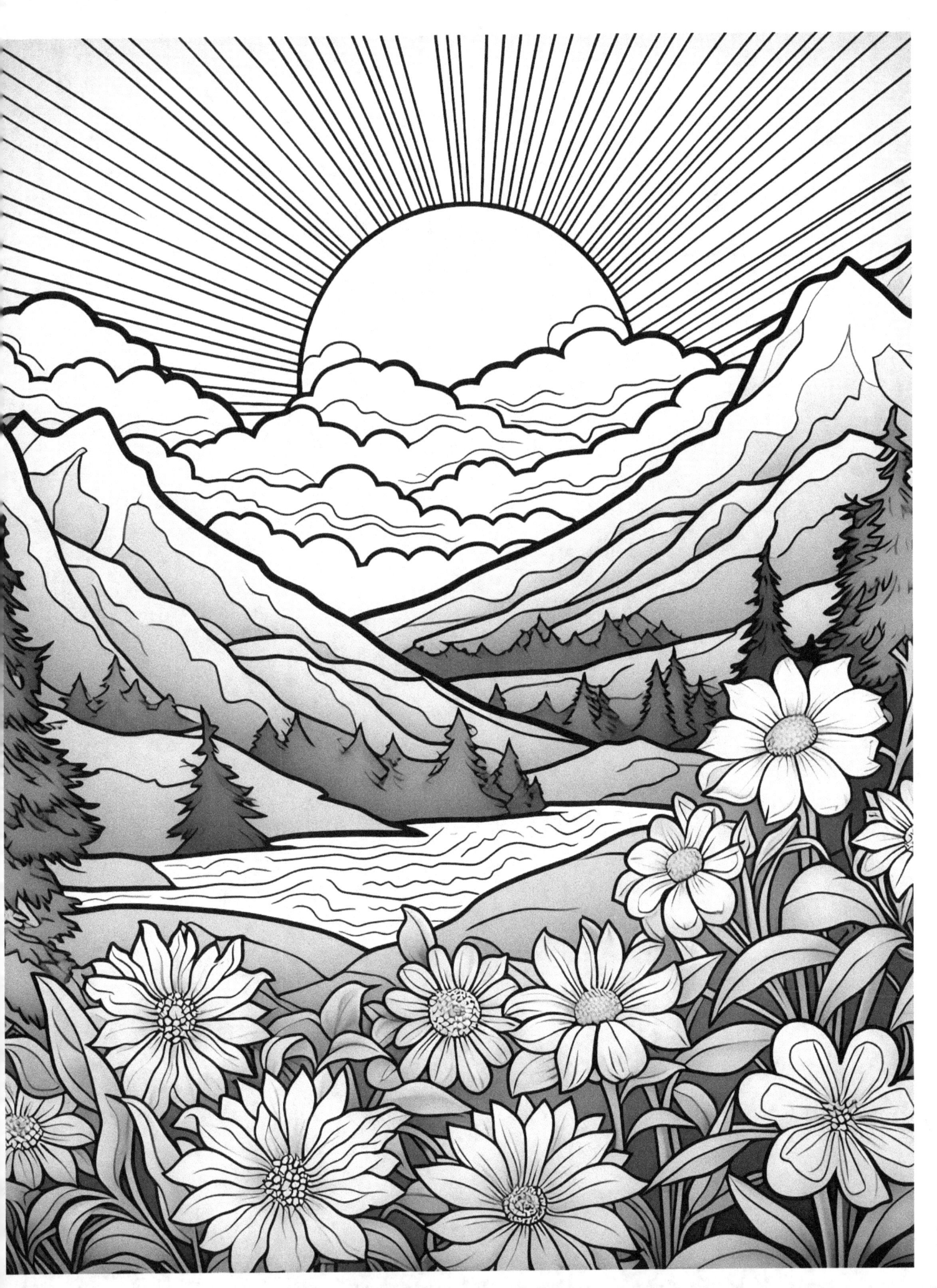

Soft candlelight's glow,

Warmth wraps in a gentle hug,

Comfort in the dark.

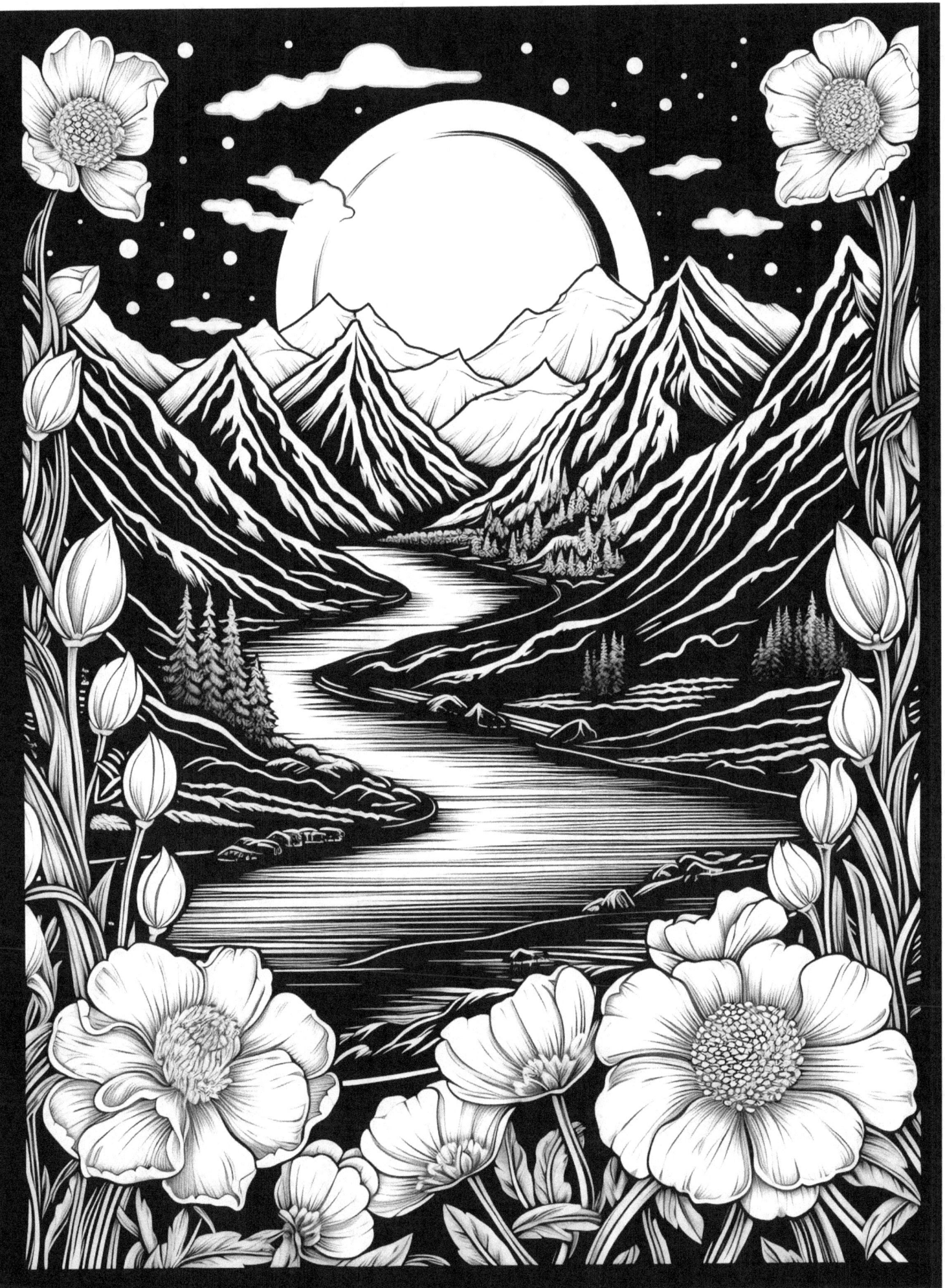

Dew on petals gleams,

Small joys in nature's details,

Gratitude whispers.

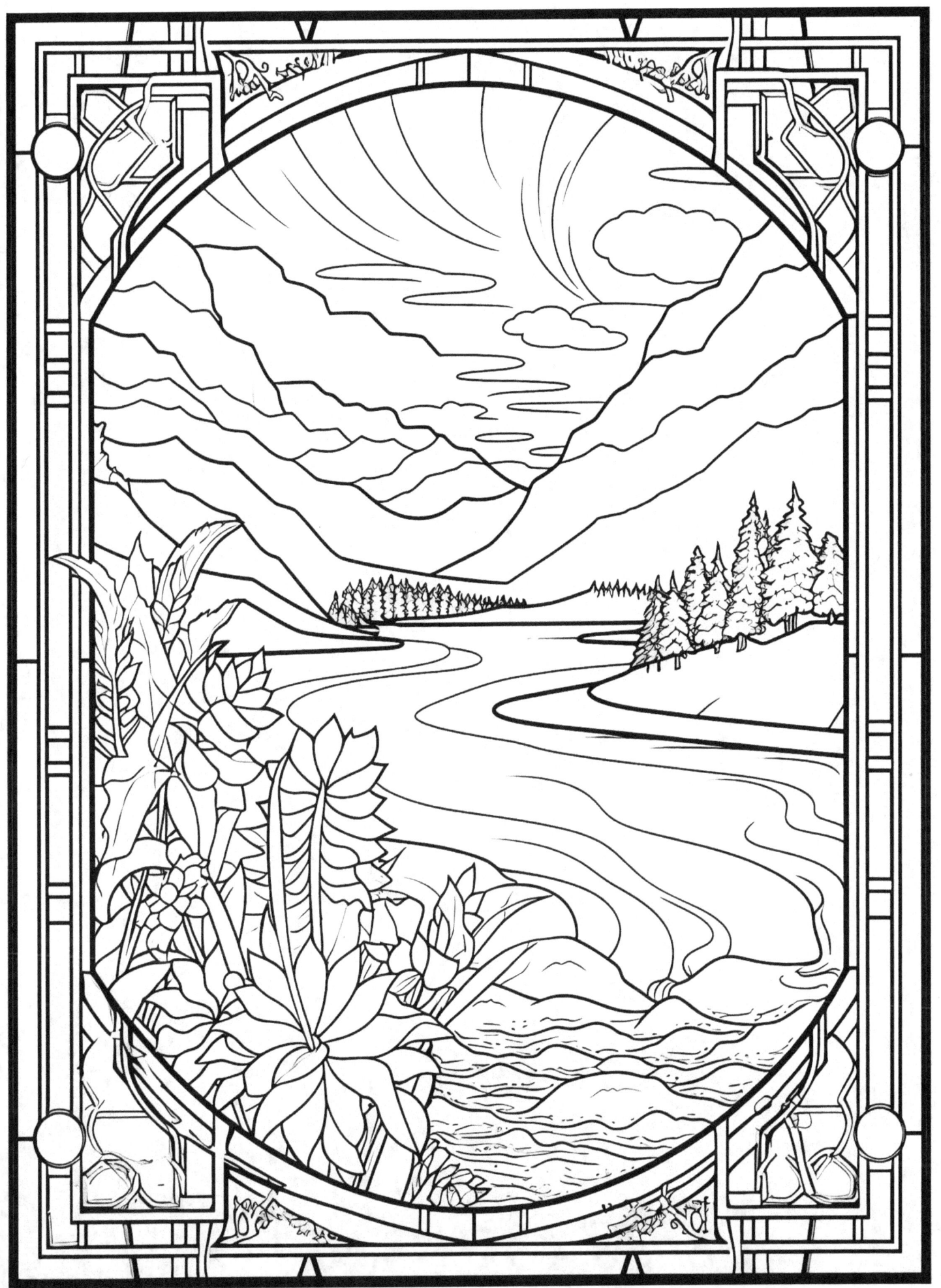

Laughter intertwines,

Kindred spirits side by side,

Best friends, hearts align.

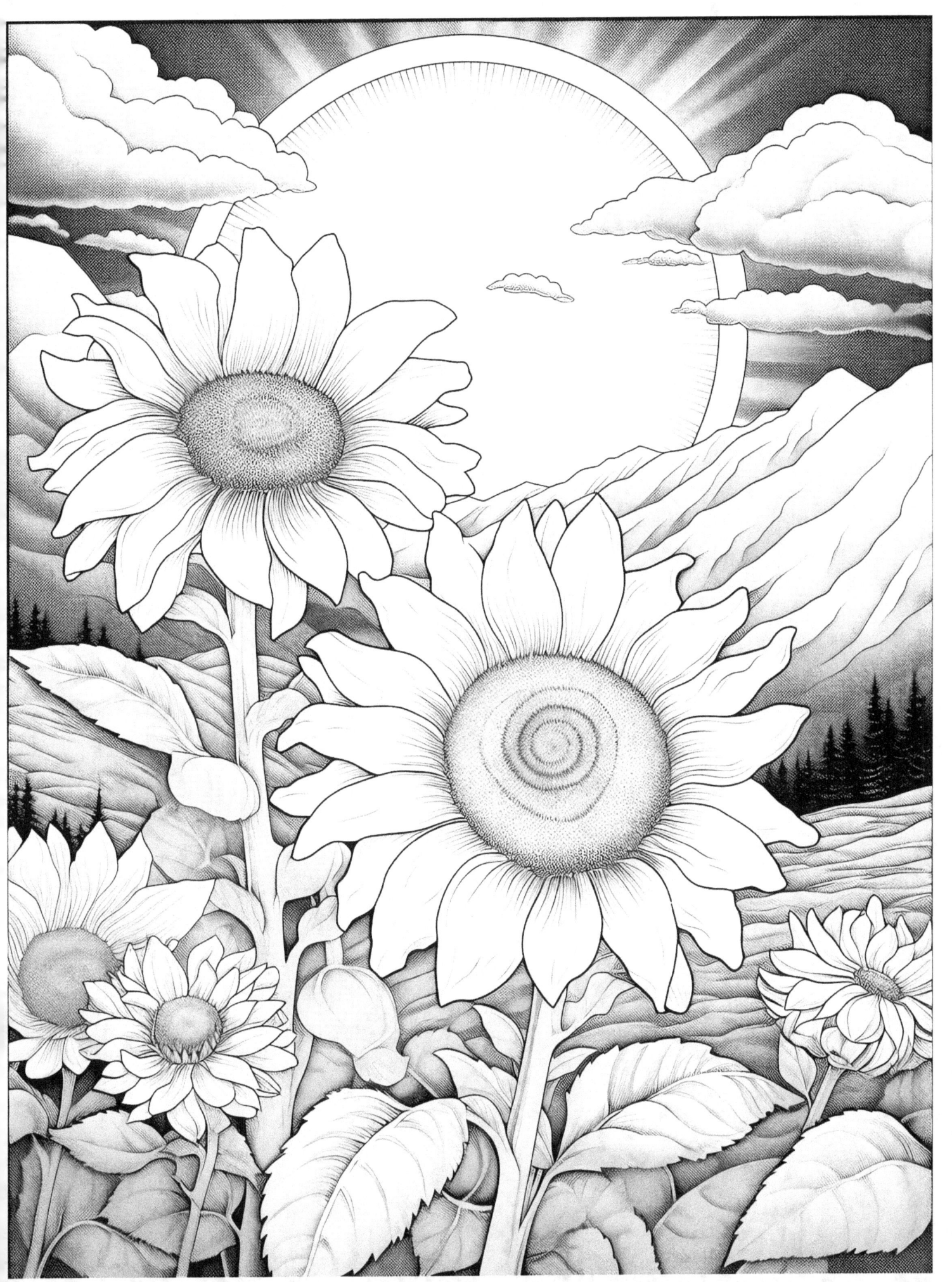

Wrinkled wisdom speaks,

Echoes of elder's journey,

Time's lessons, cherished.

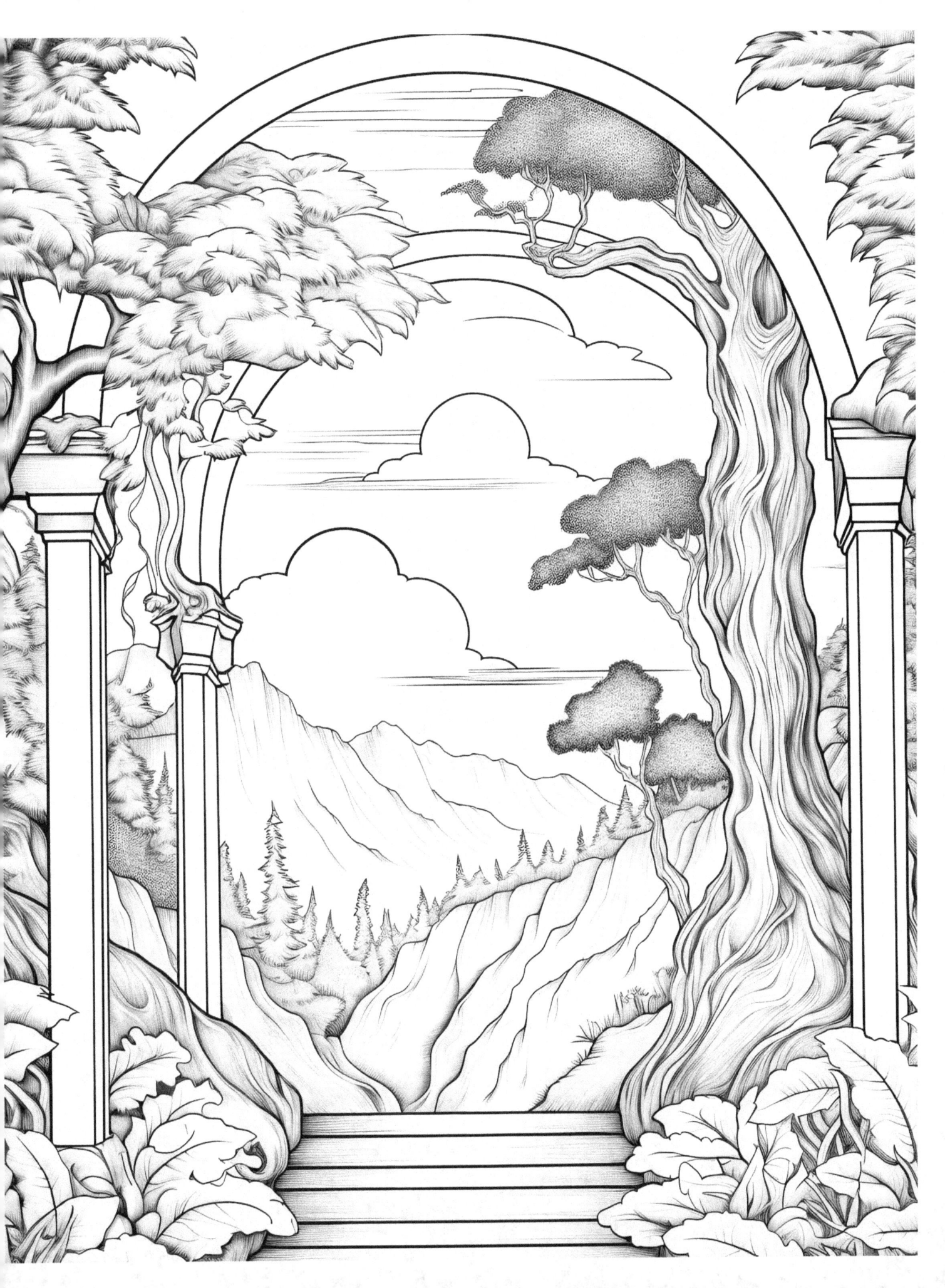

Starry canvas vast,

Silent reflections unfold,

Universe whispers.

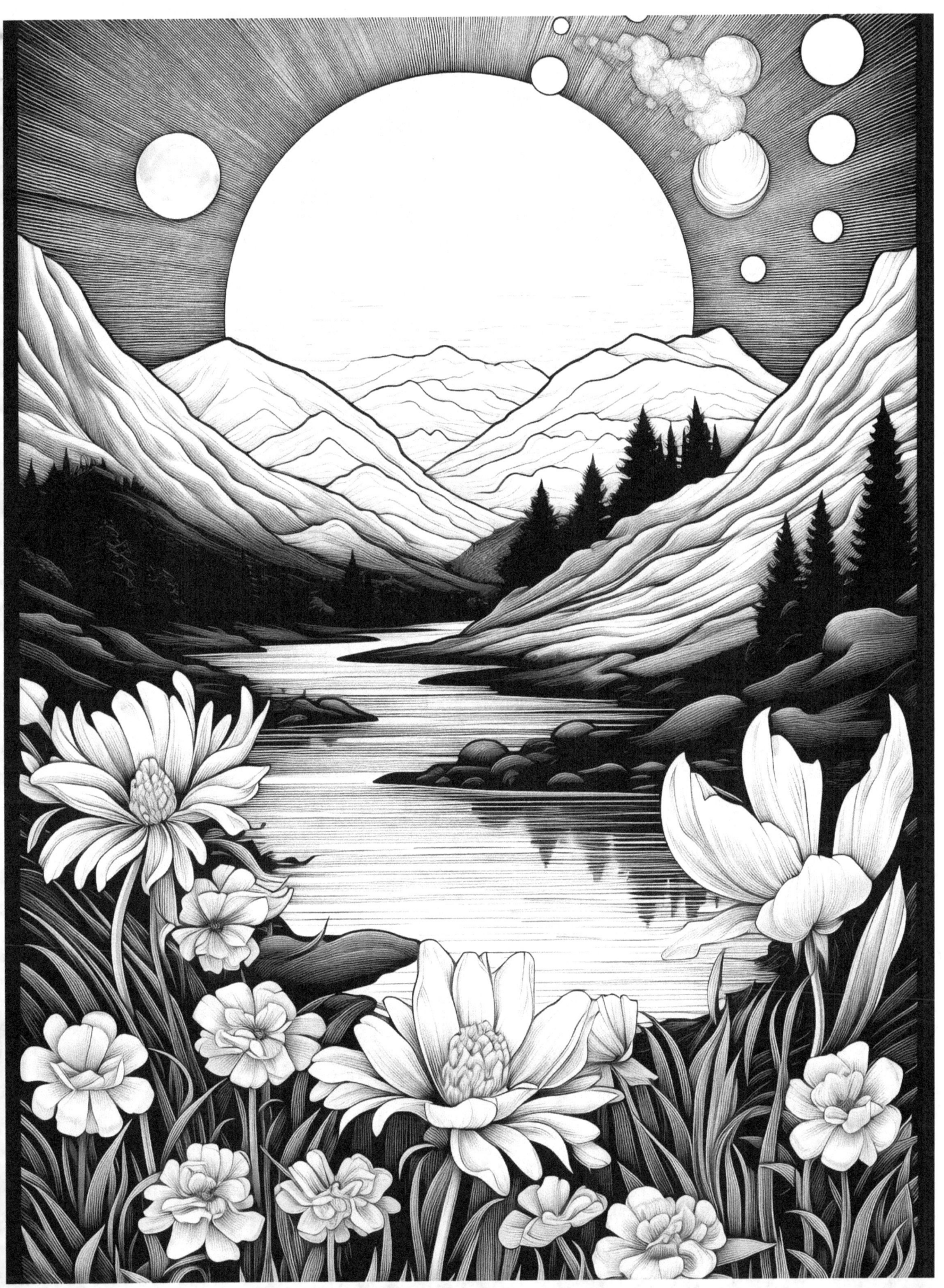

River's gentle flow,

Navigating currents right,

Destiny in stream.

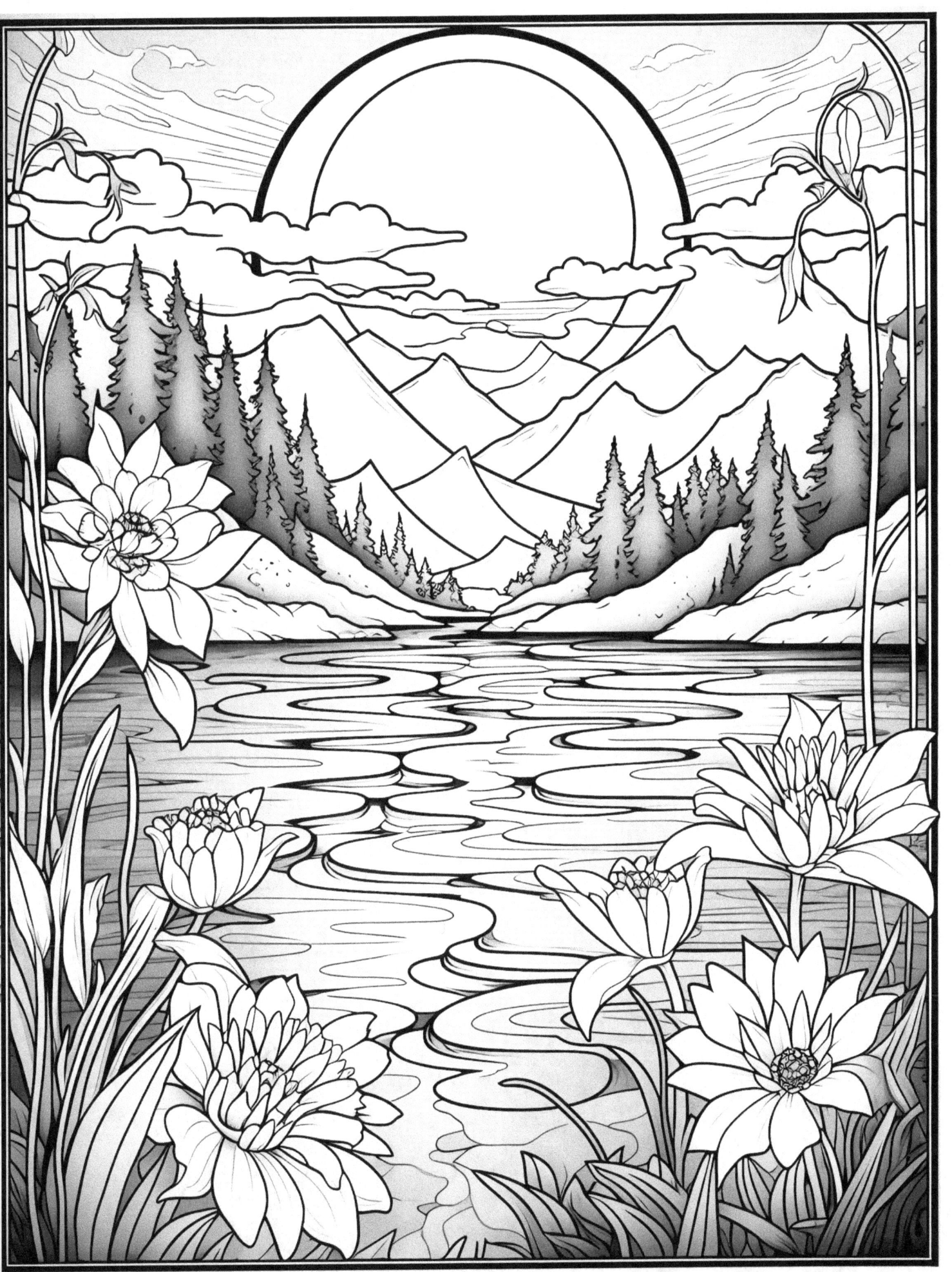

Forest whispers call,

Hiking trails unveil beauty,

Nature's embrace blooms.

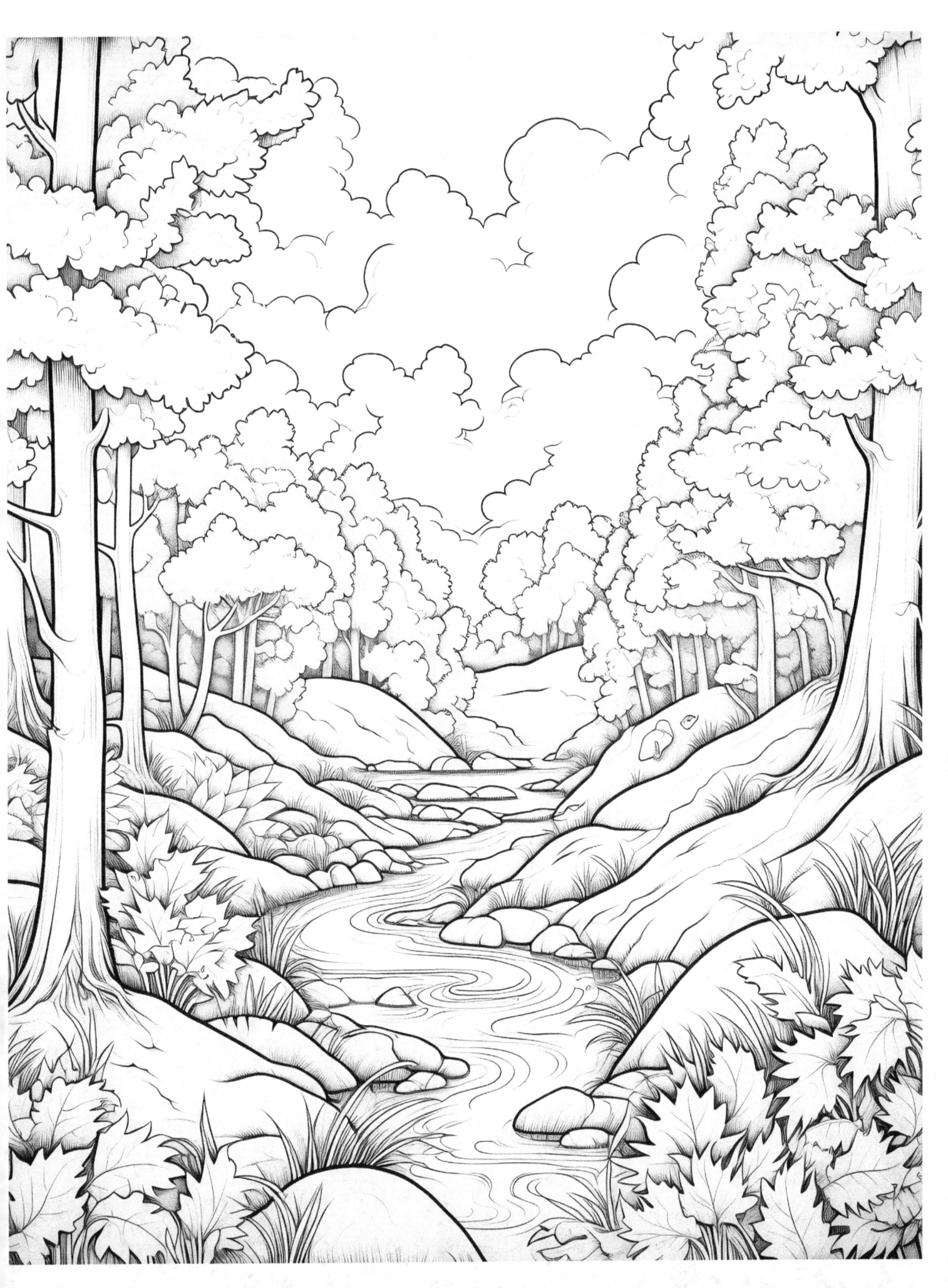

Storm clouds parting ways,

Sunlight pierces, paints the sky,

Hope in clearing storms.

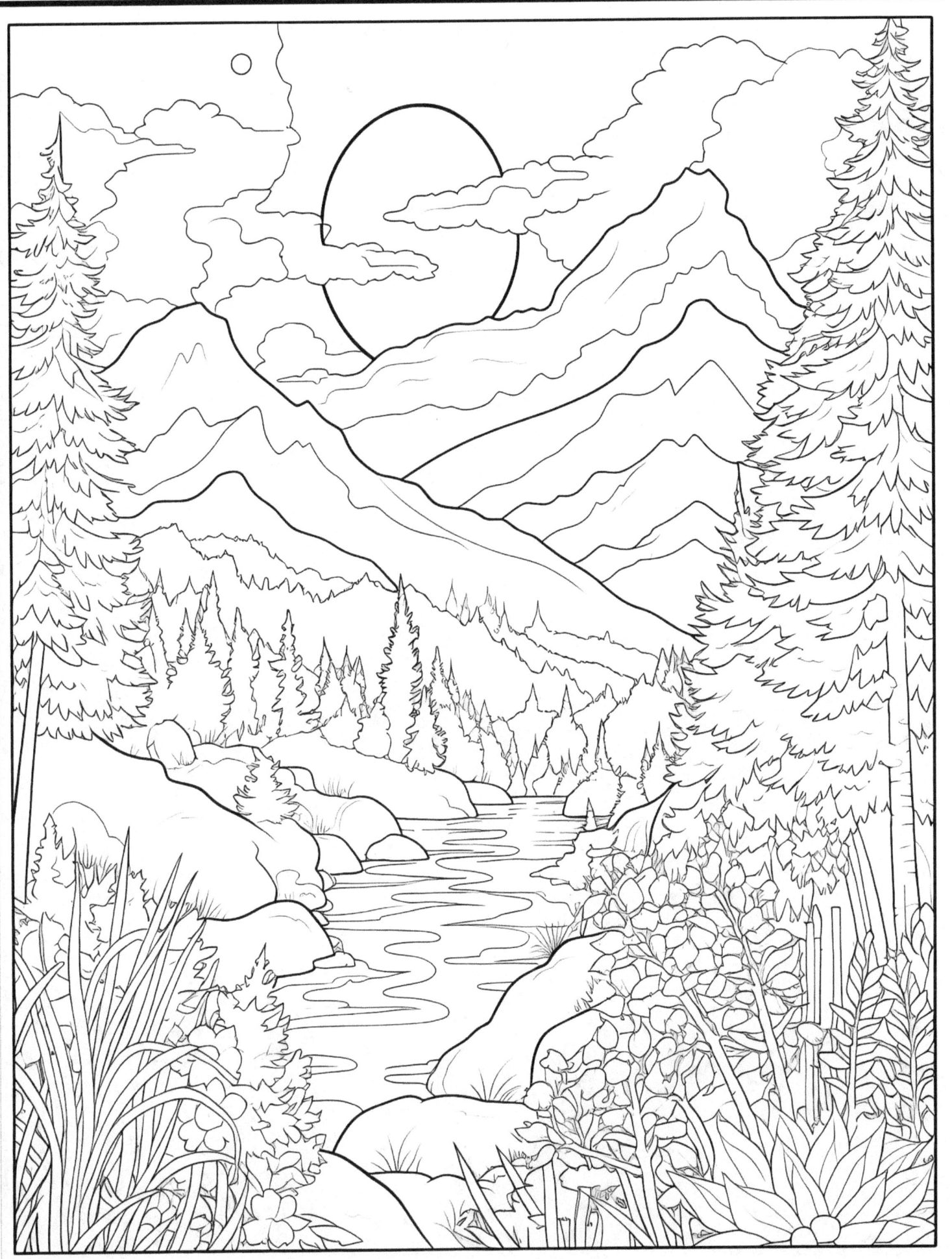

Organized realms thrive,

Every piece finds its own place,

Order's gentle rule.

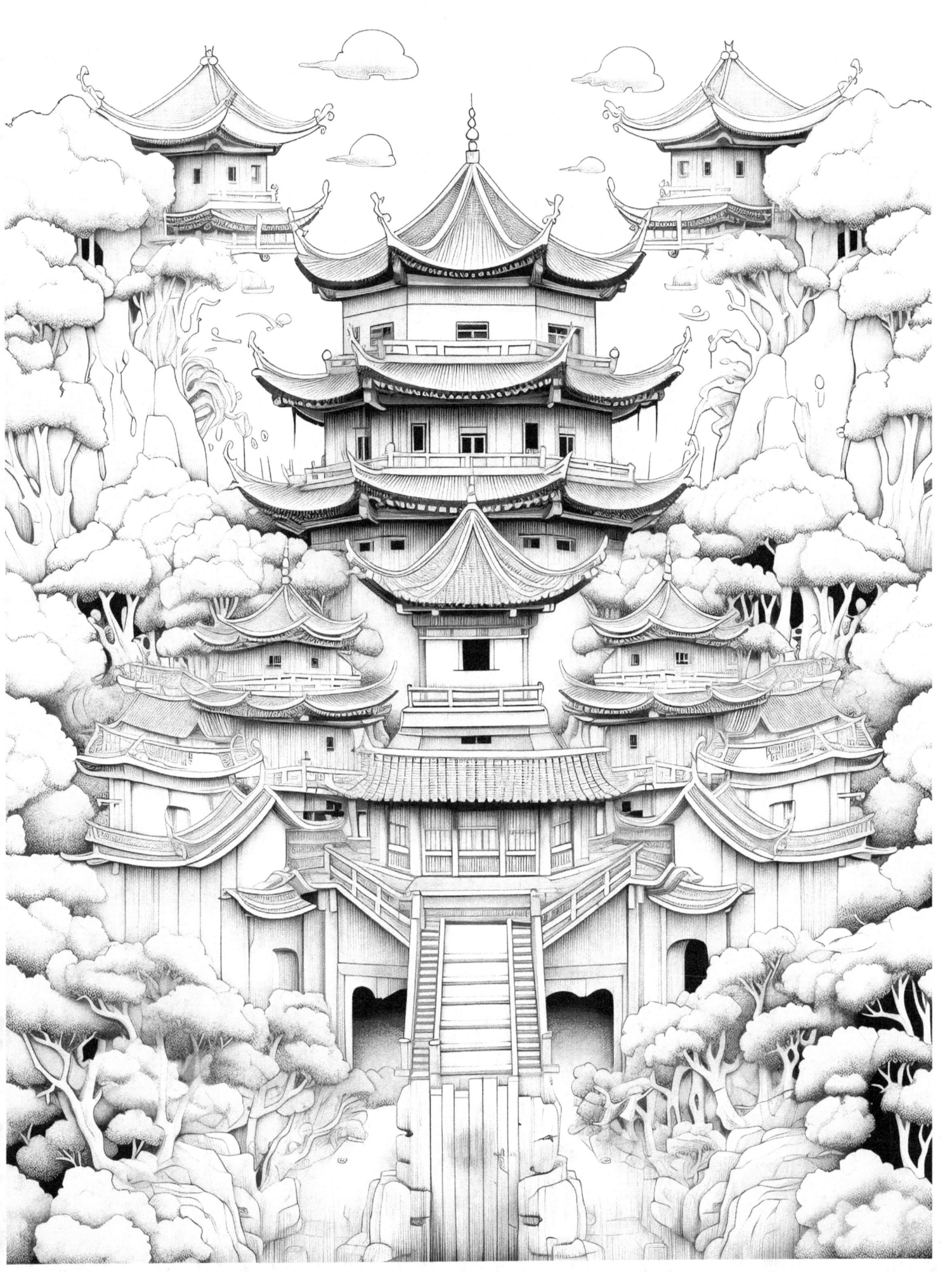

Challenges, like peaks,

Beauty in ascent's trials,

Strength in every step.

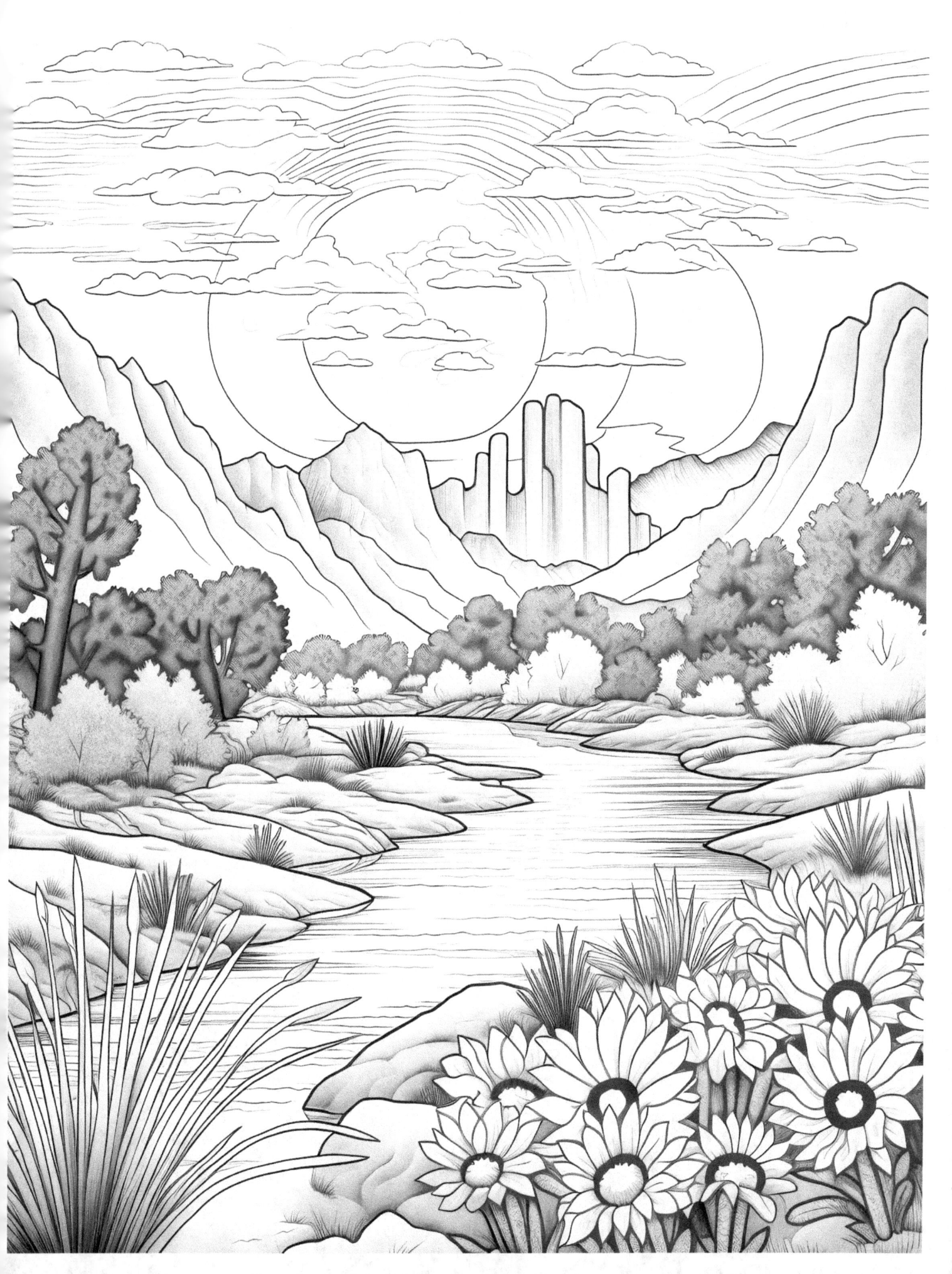

Vast dreams paint the sky,

Big visions, stars in our eyes,

Possibilities.

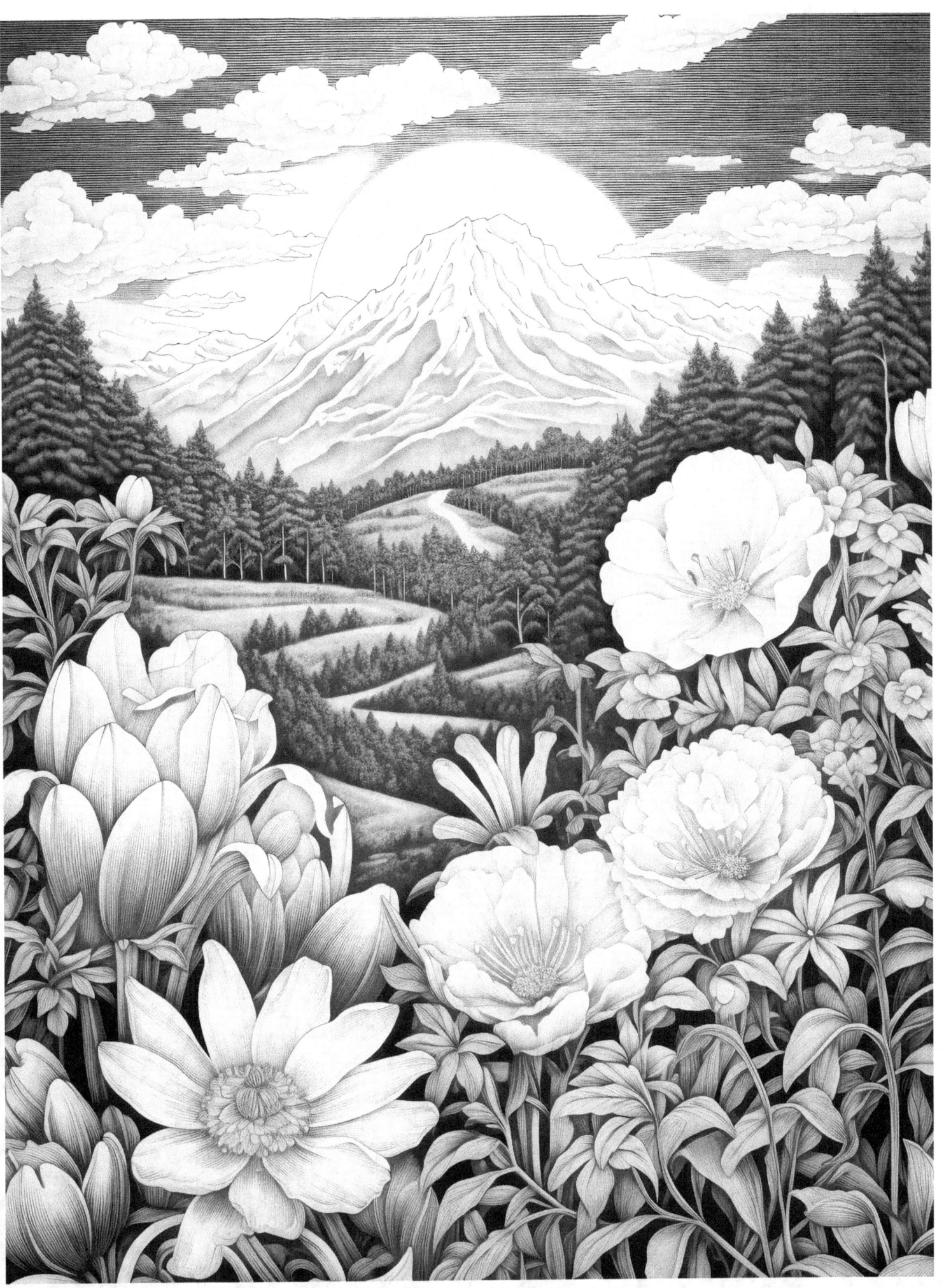

Footsteps on life's path,

Journey's rhythm in each stride,

Destiny unfolds.

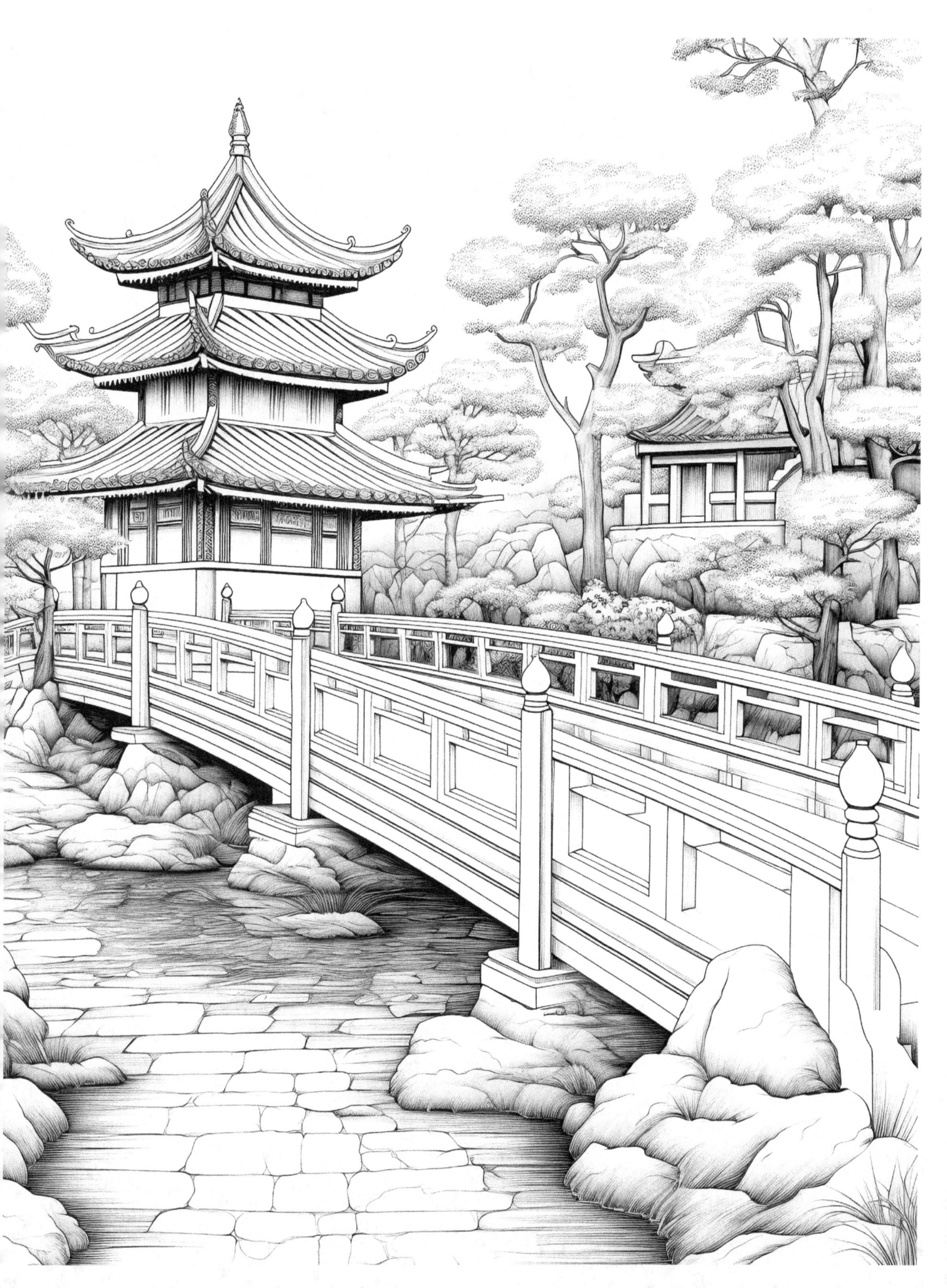

Uncharted land calls,

Bold footsteps carve paths unseen,

Trailblazing echoes.

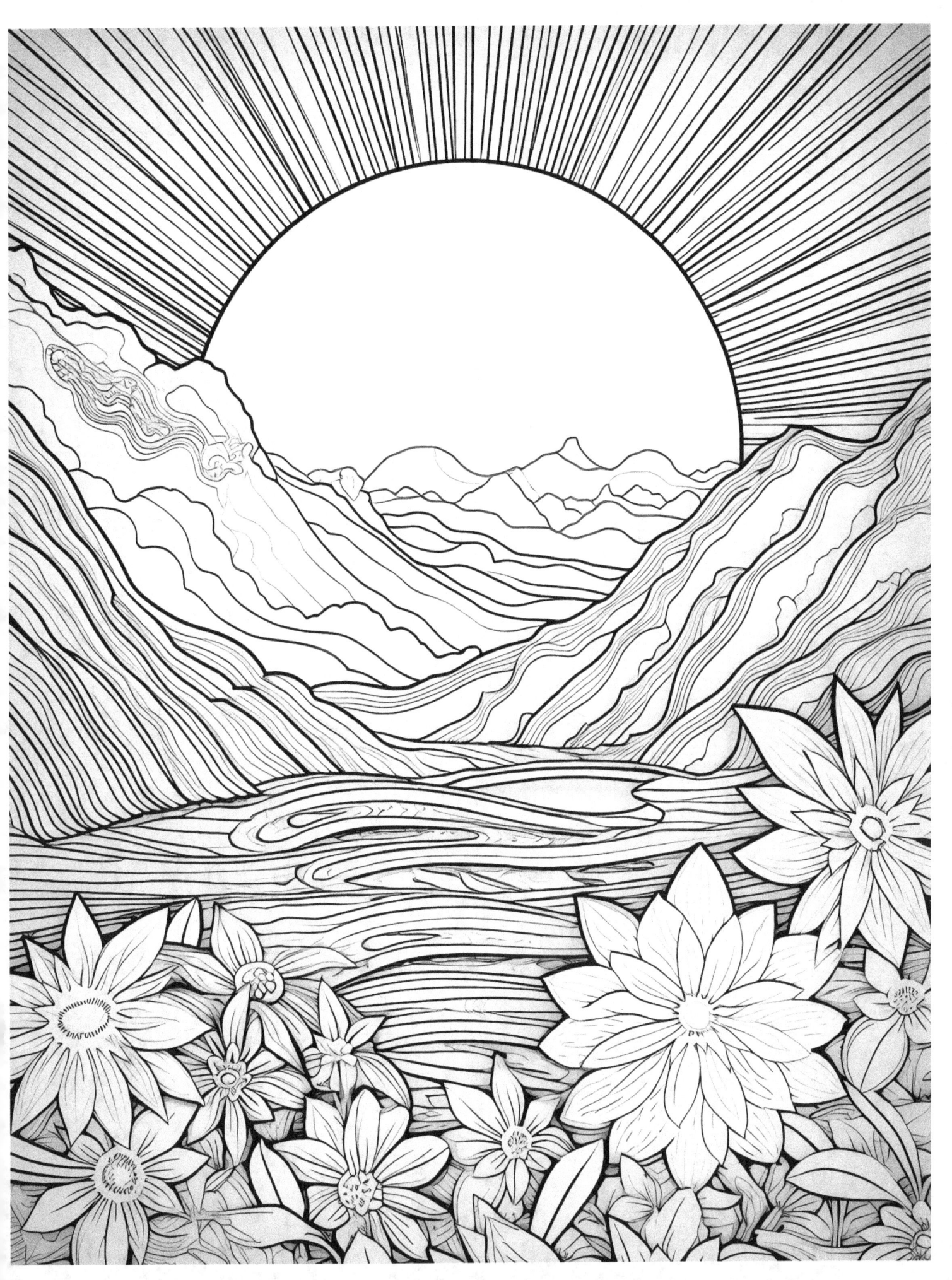

Sun's warm tender kiss,

Golden rays embrace the soul,

Basking in pure light.

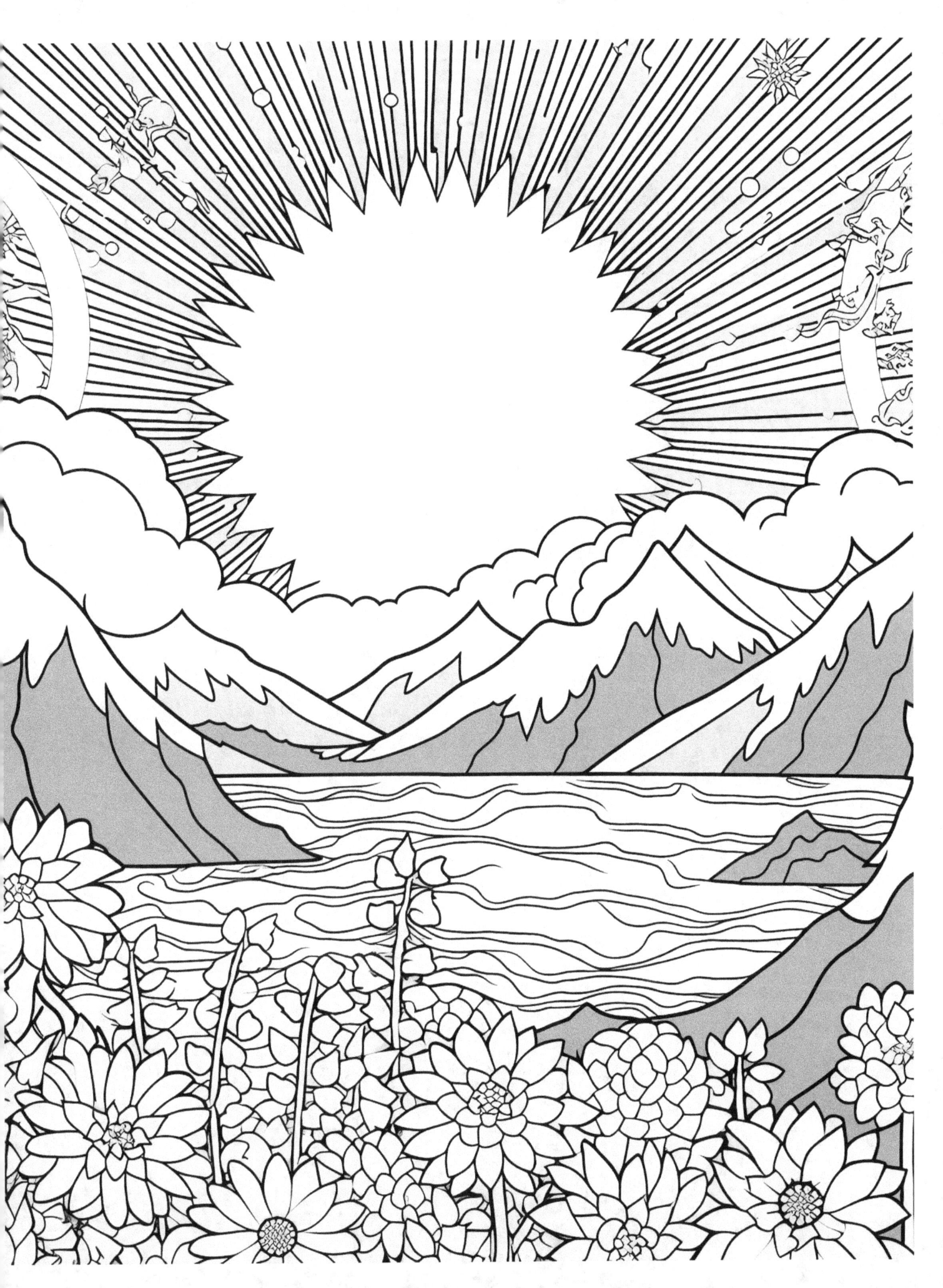

Amidst peers, a star,

Individual light shines,

Distinct, yet embraced.

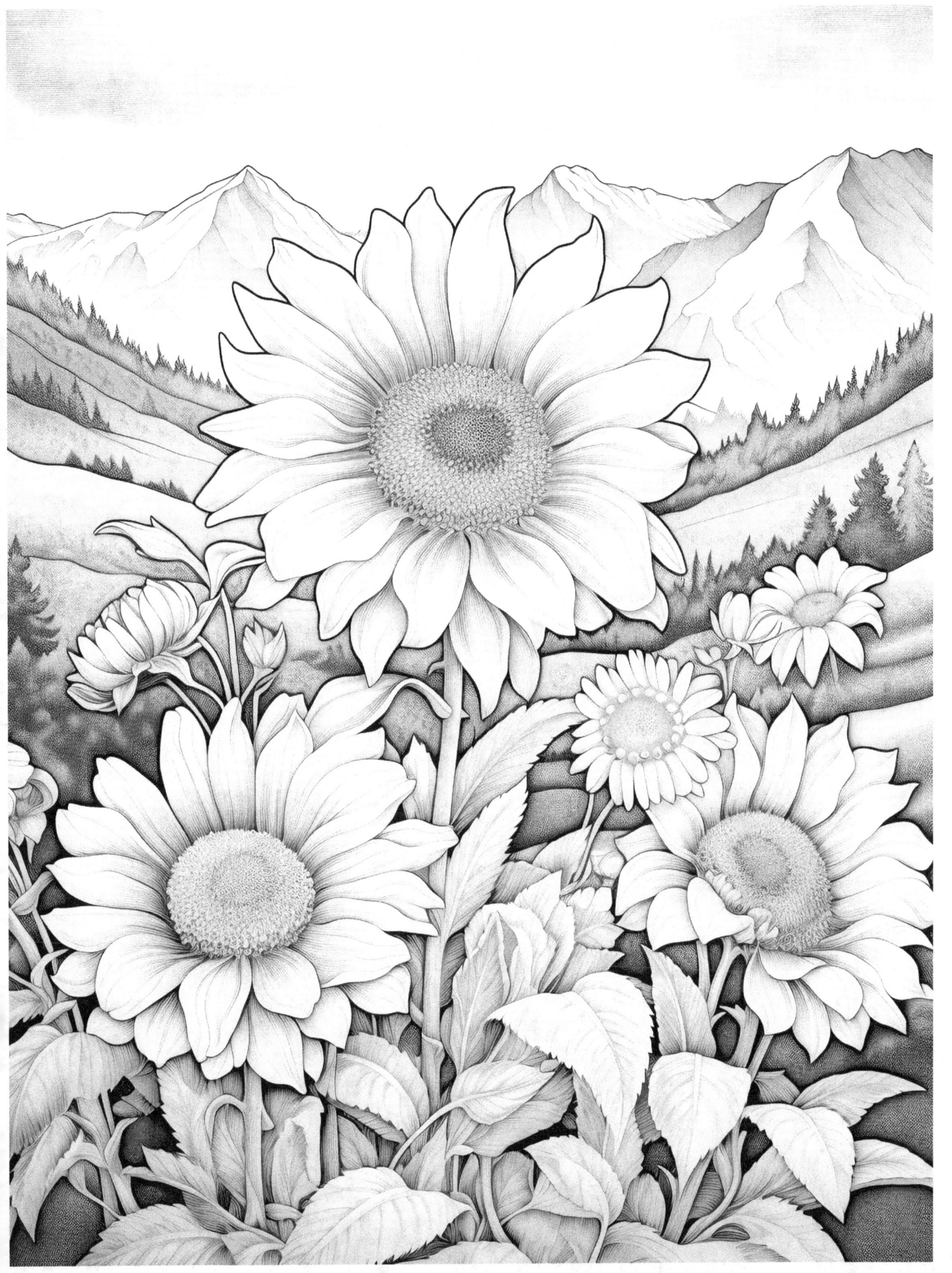

Rugged terrain speaks,

Streams of resilience carve through,

Nature's strength unveiled.

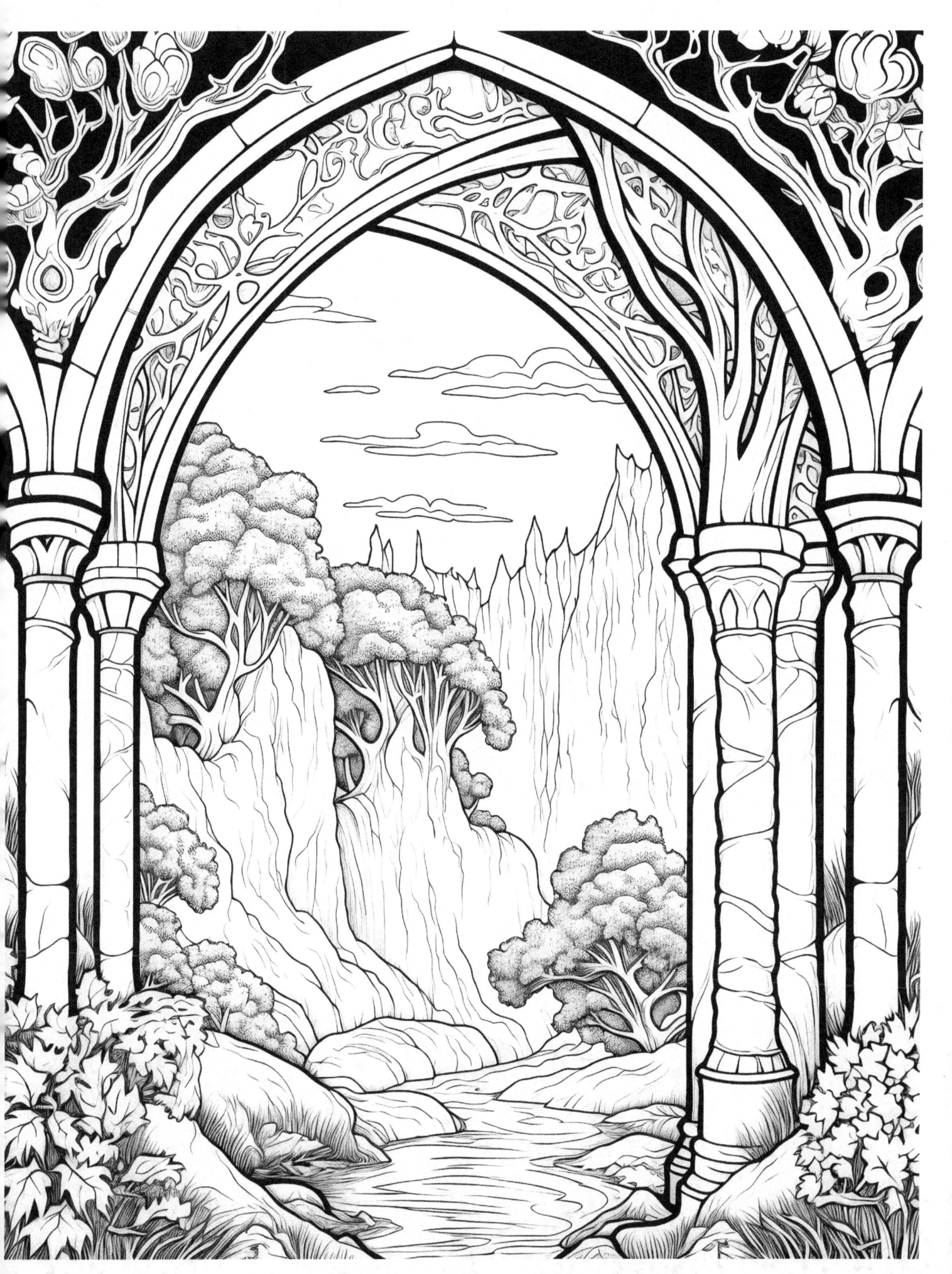

Whispers in the breeze,

Humans dance with nature's grace,

Coexistence blooms.

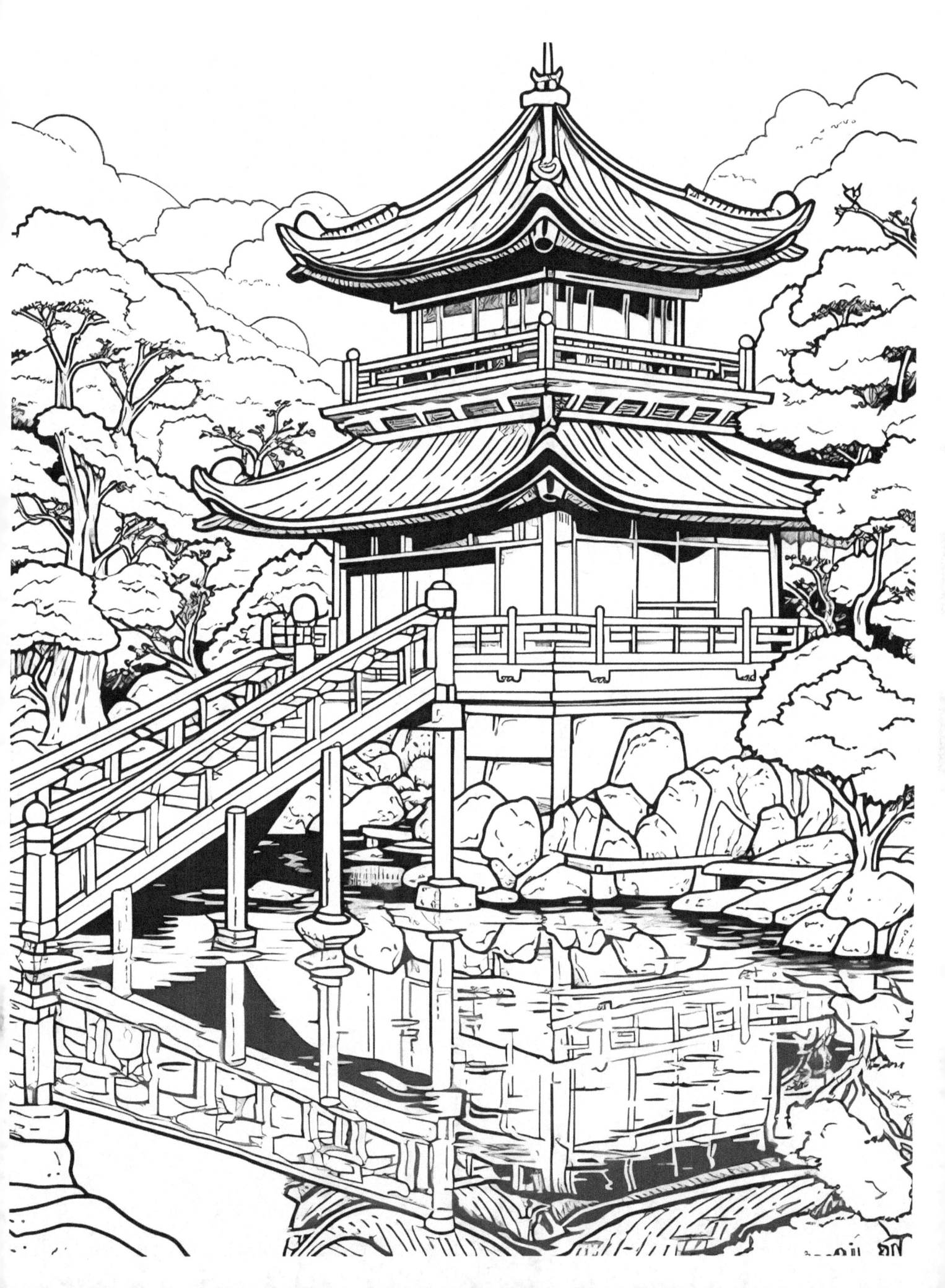

Rushing waters sing,

Courage carves a winding path,

Swift currents embraced.

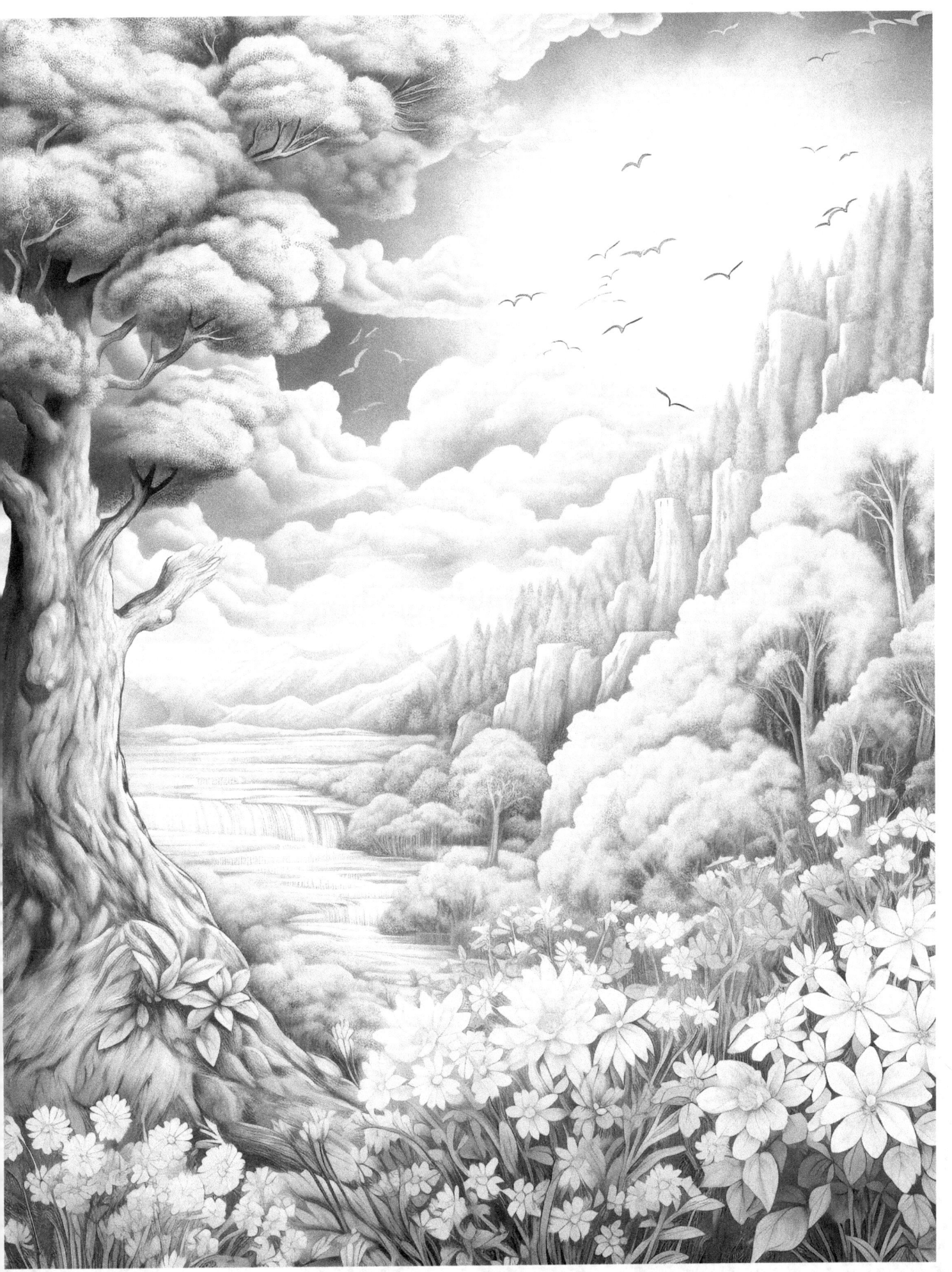

Rapids left behind,

Calm waters cradle the soul,

Tranquil ripples soothe.

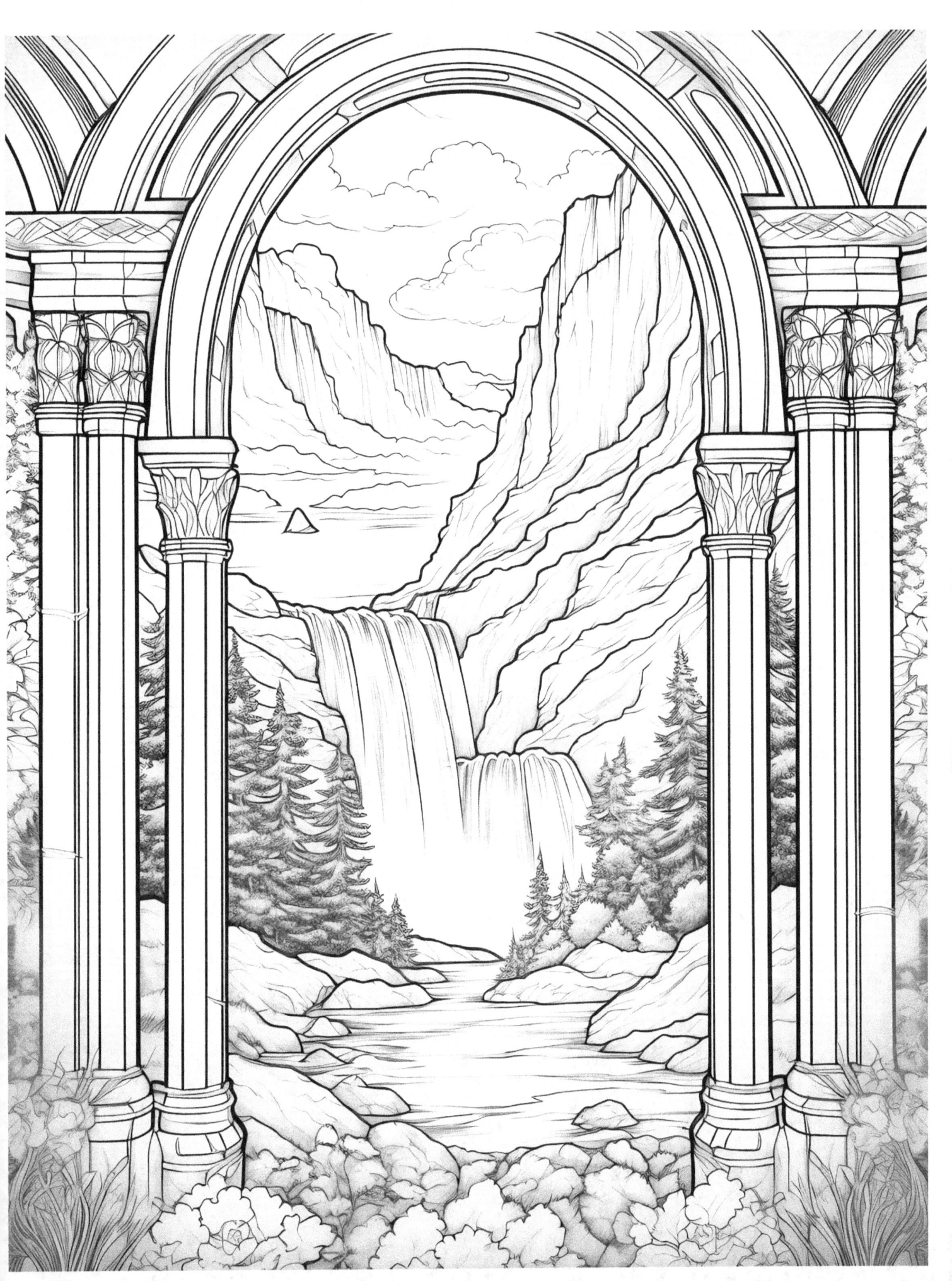

Clutter fades away,

Inner compass points the way,

Clear path, purpose found.

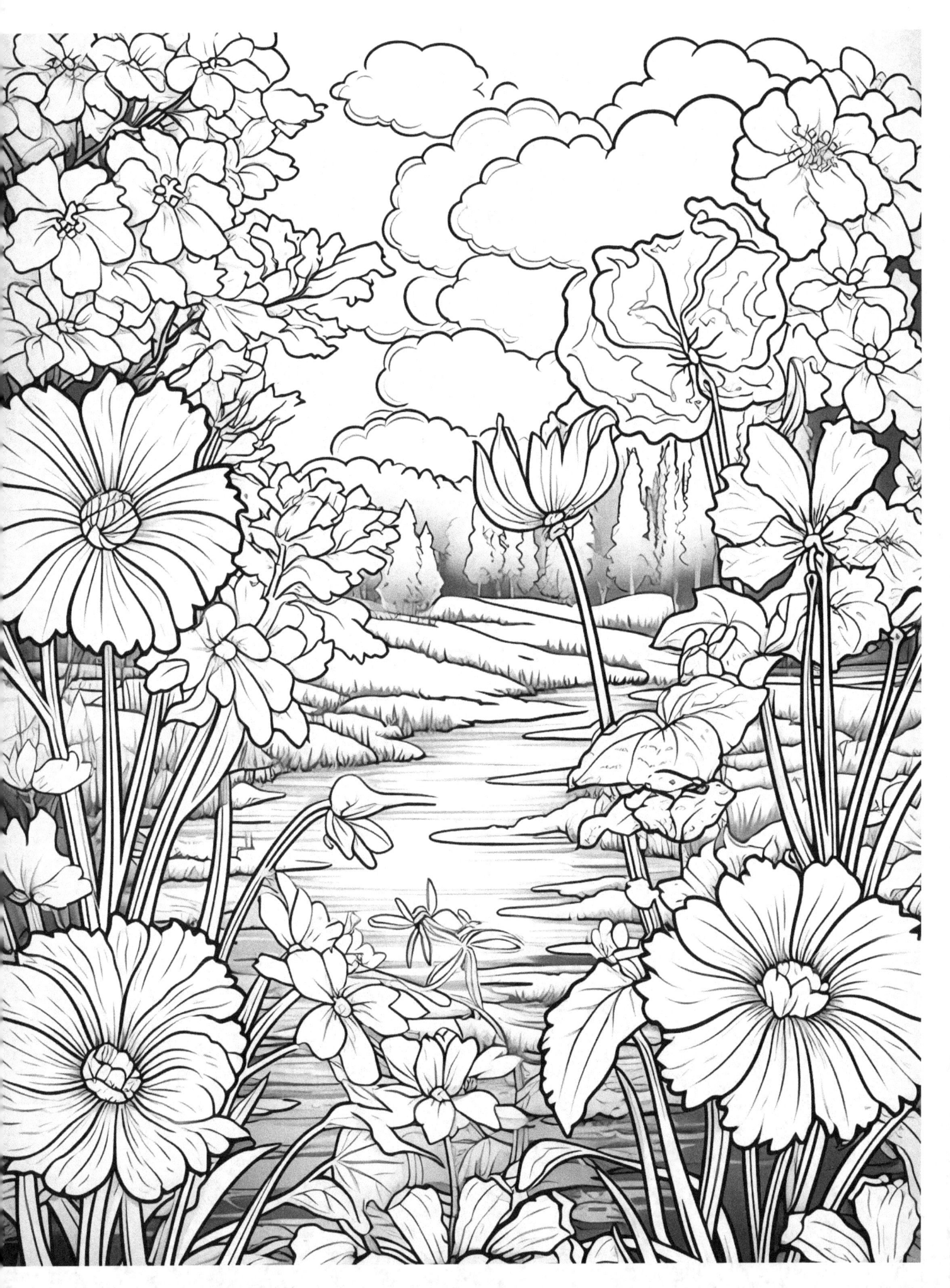

Still waters run deep,

Silent echoes of triumph,

Reflecting success.

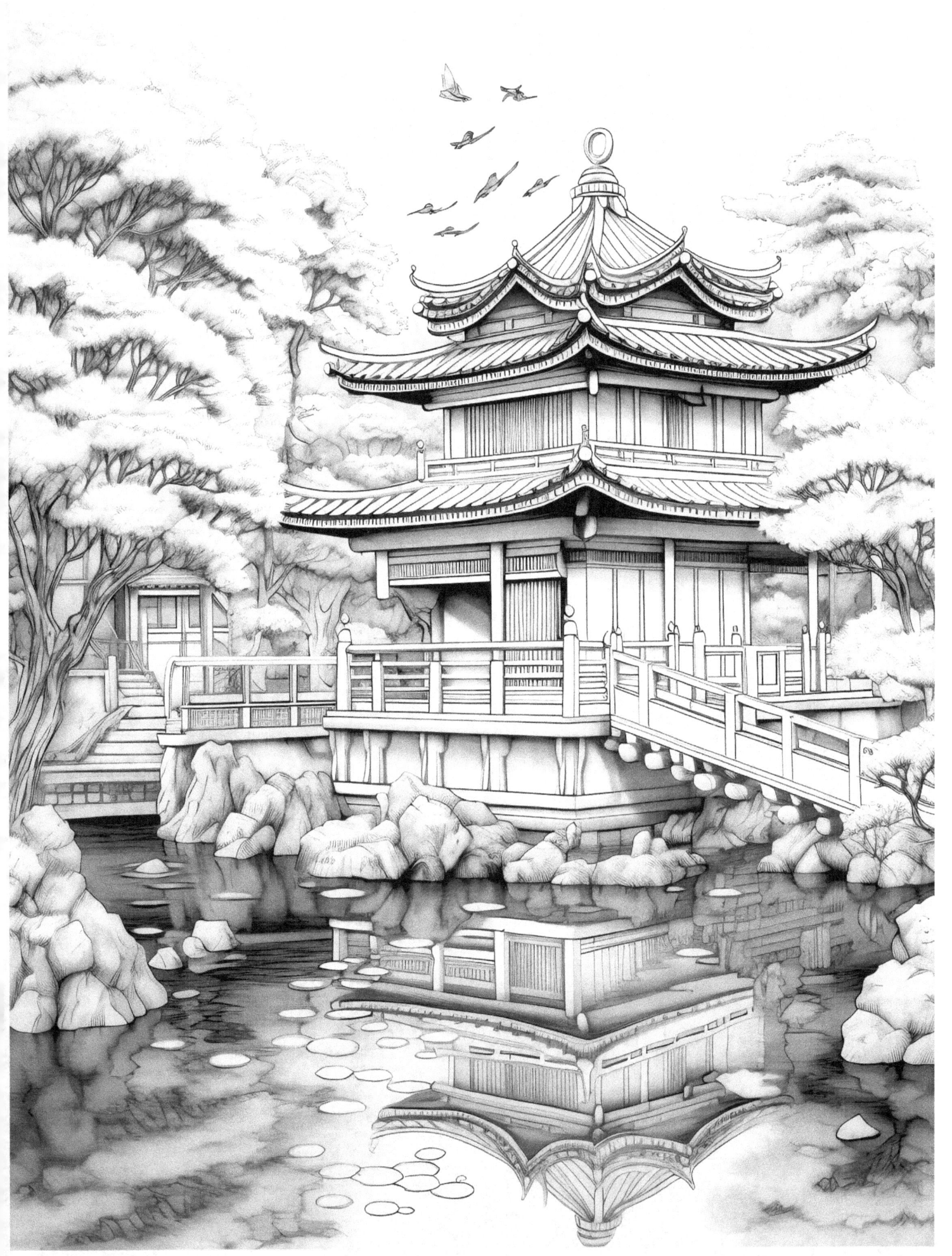

Through trials, rebirth,

Self-discovery unfolds,

Strength found in the scars.

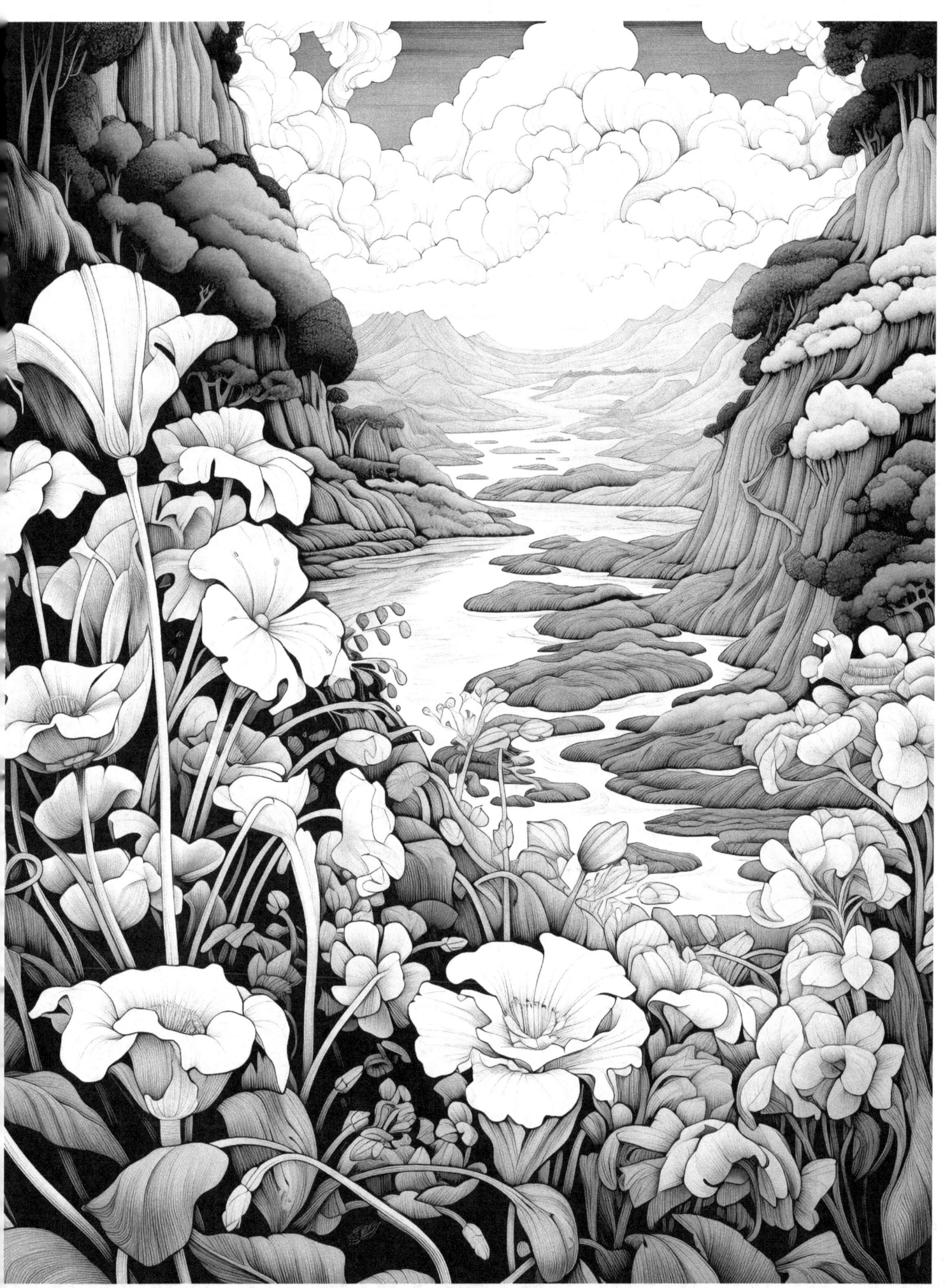

Roots in earth's embrace,

Reflect, honor origin,

Strength in grounded past.

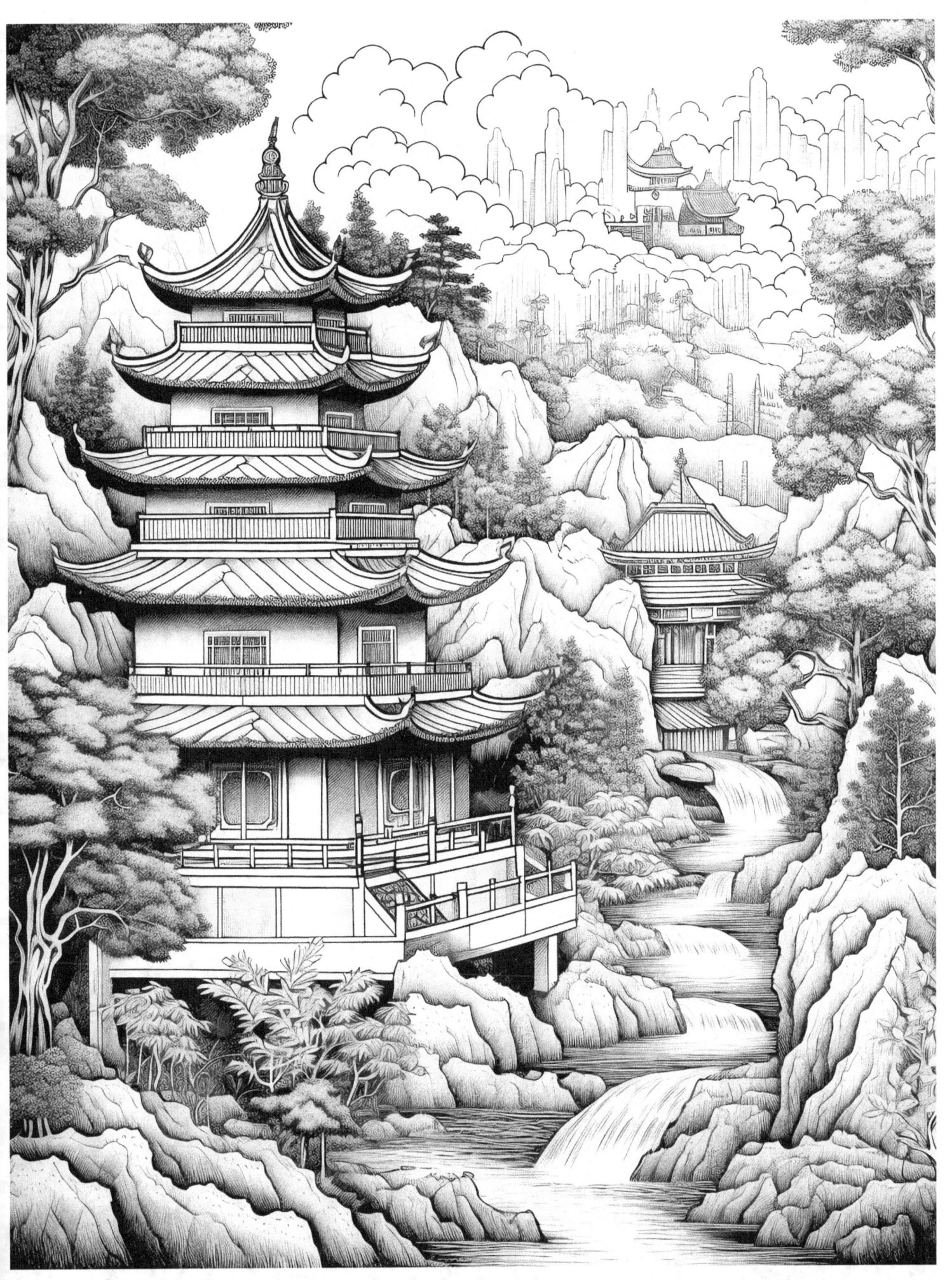

Melody of peace,

Harmony in life's embrace,

Soul's symphony sings.

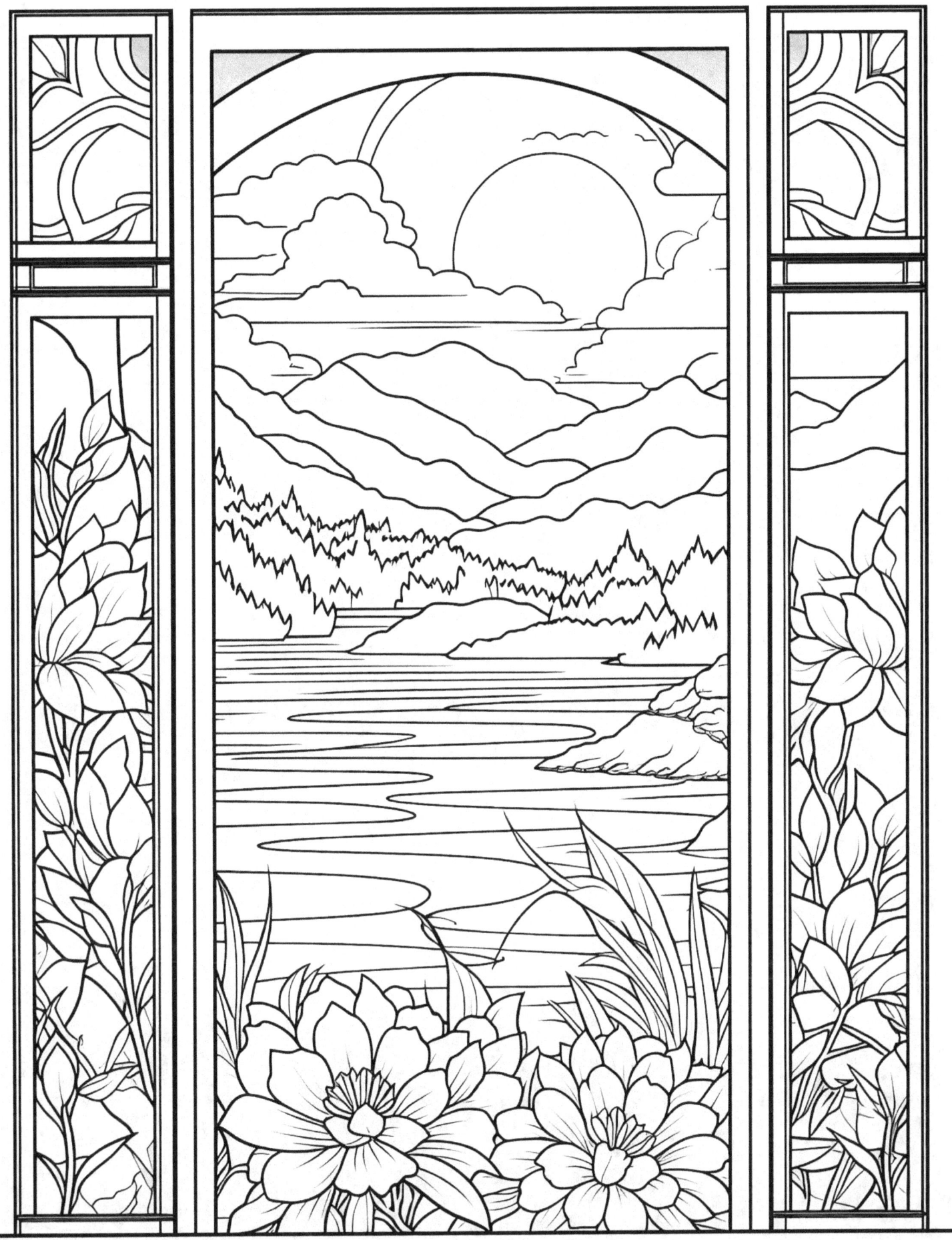

Silent peace descends,

Moments wrapped in calm repose,

Joy in stillness found.

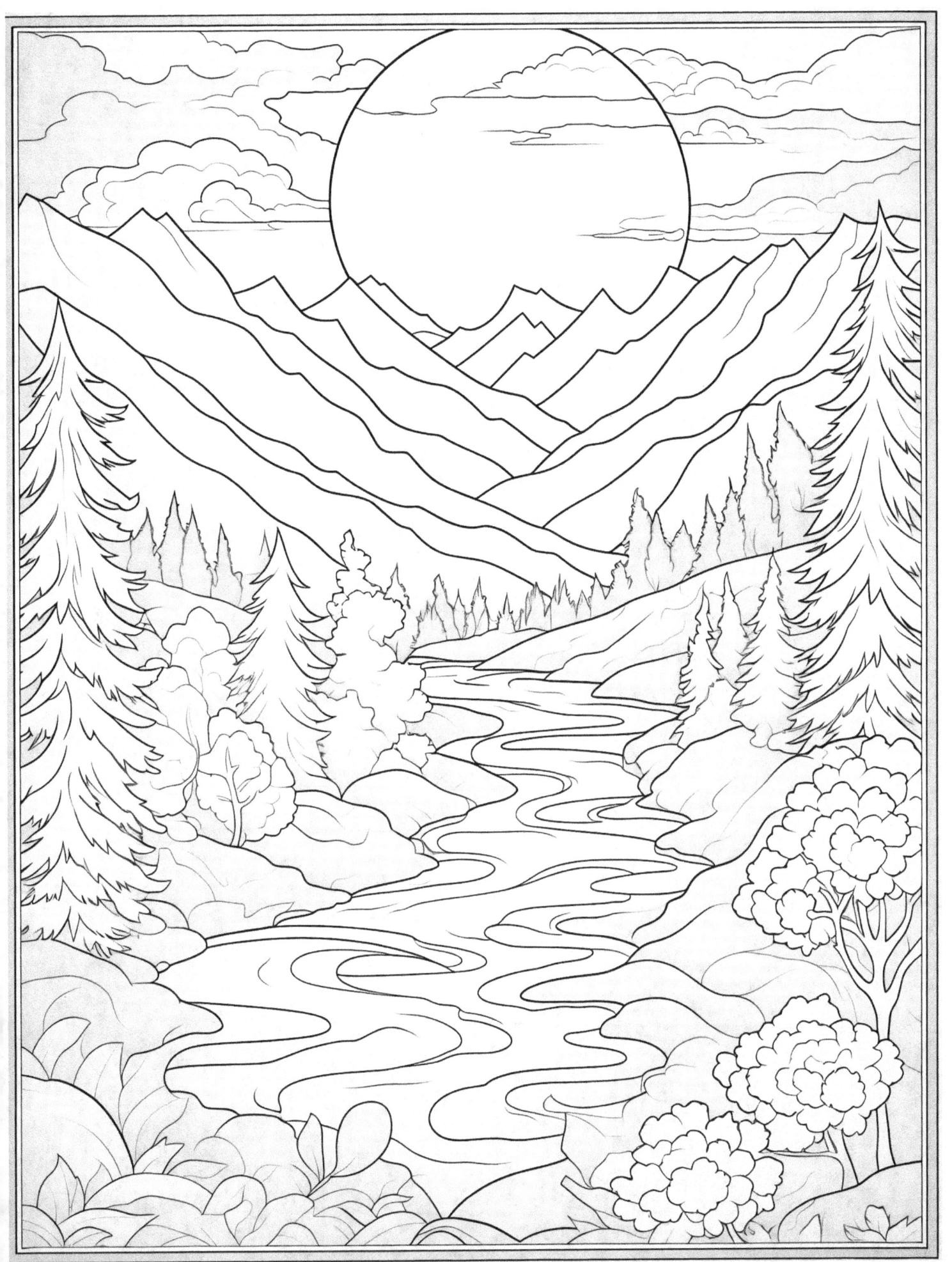

Embrace of old friends,

Laughter echoes through the years,

Reunion's warmth blooms.

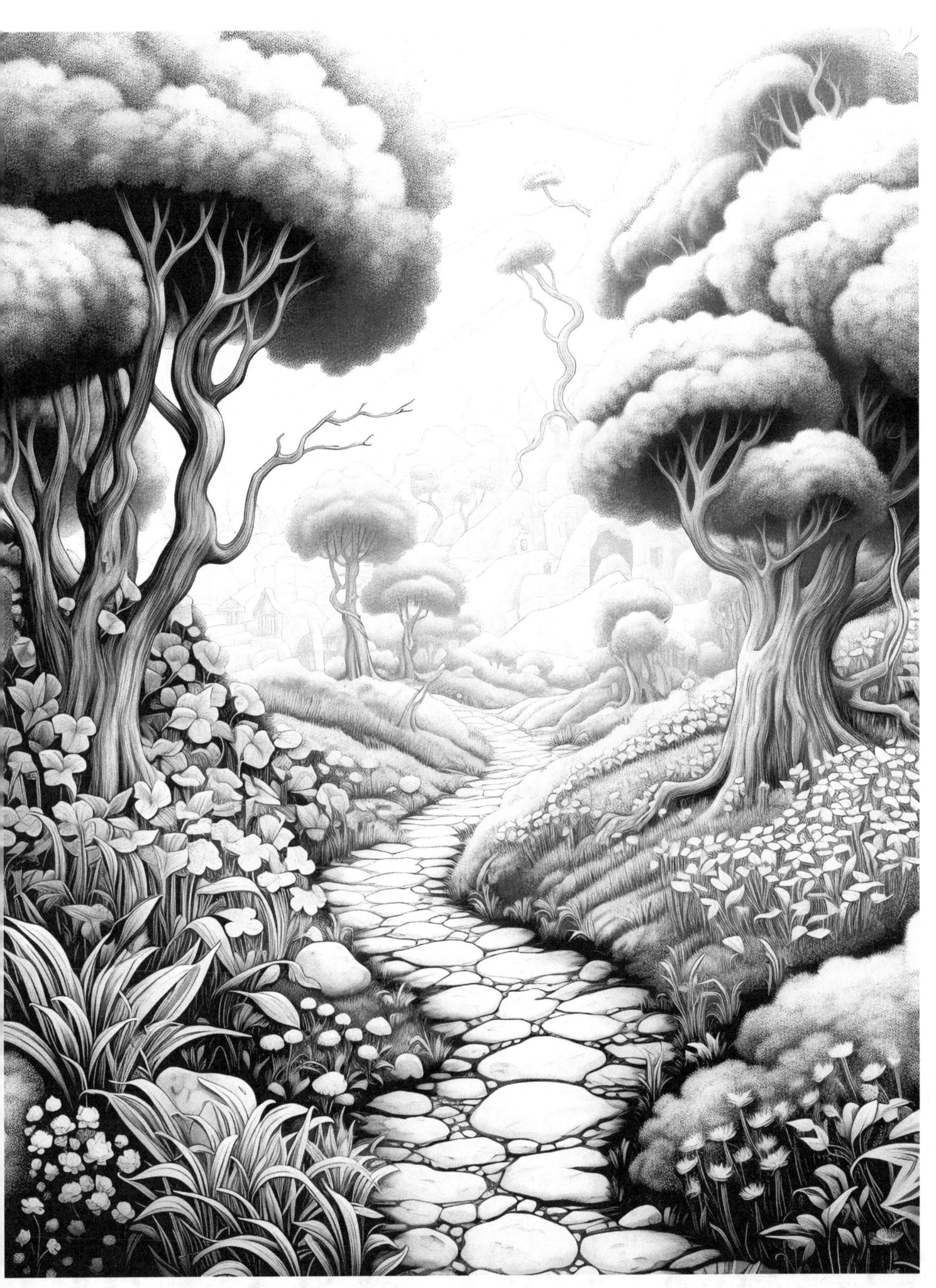

Full moon's silver glow,

Night's comfort in gentle beams,

Lunar embrace soothes.

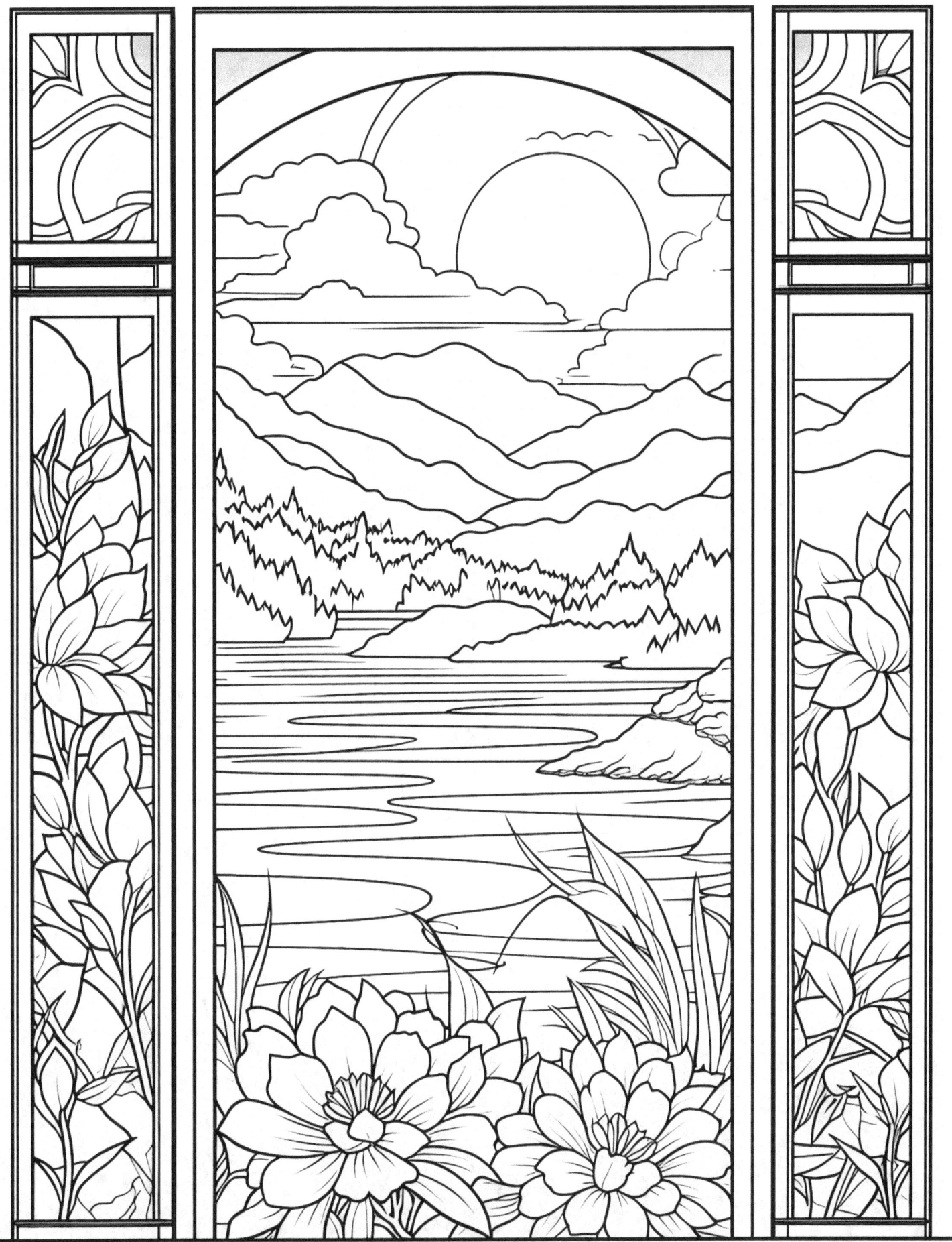

Paths before me stretch,

Choices bloom at journey's start,

Home's echo, a guide.

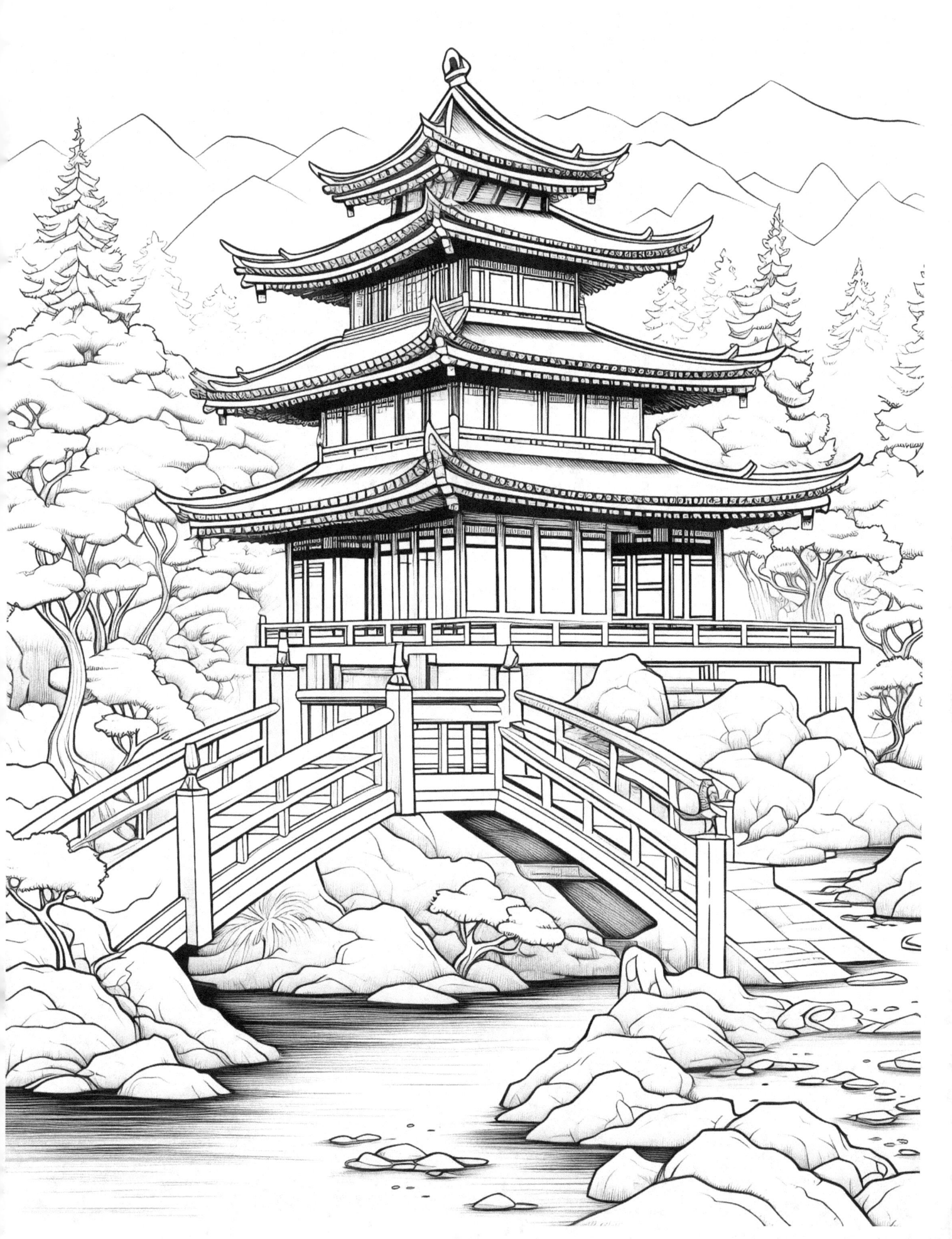

Sun's warm tender light,

Nurturing rays kiss the earth,

Life awakens, thrives.

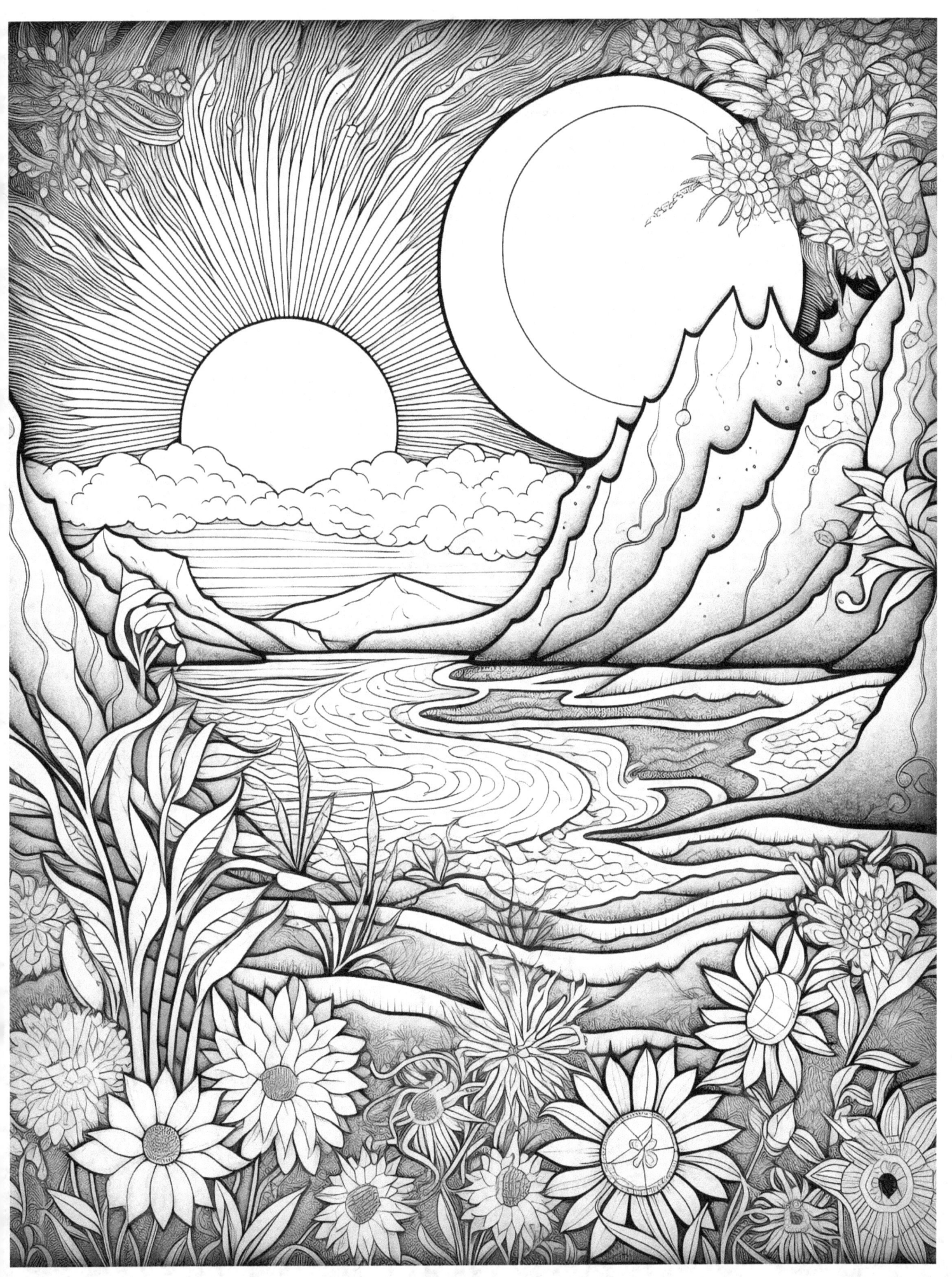

City's hum retreats,

Nature's refuge whispers peace,

Escape, green embrace.

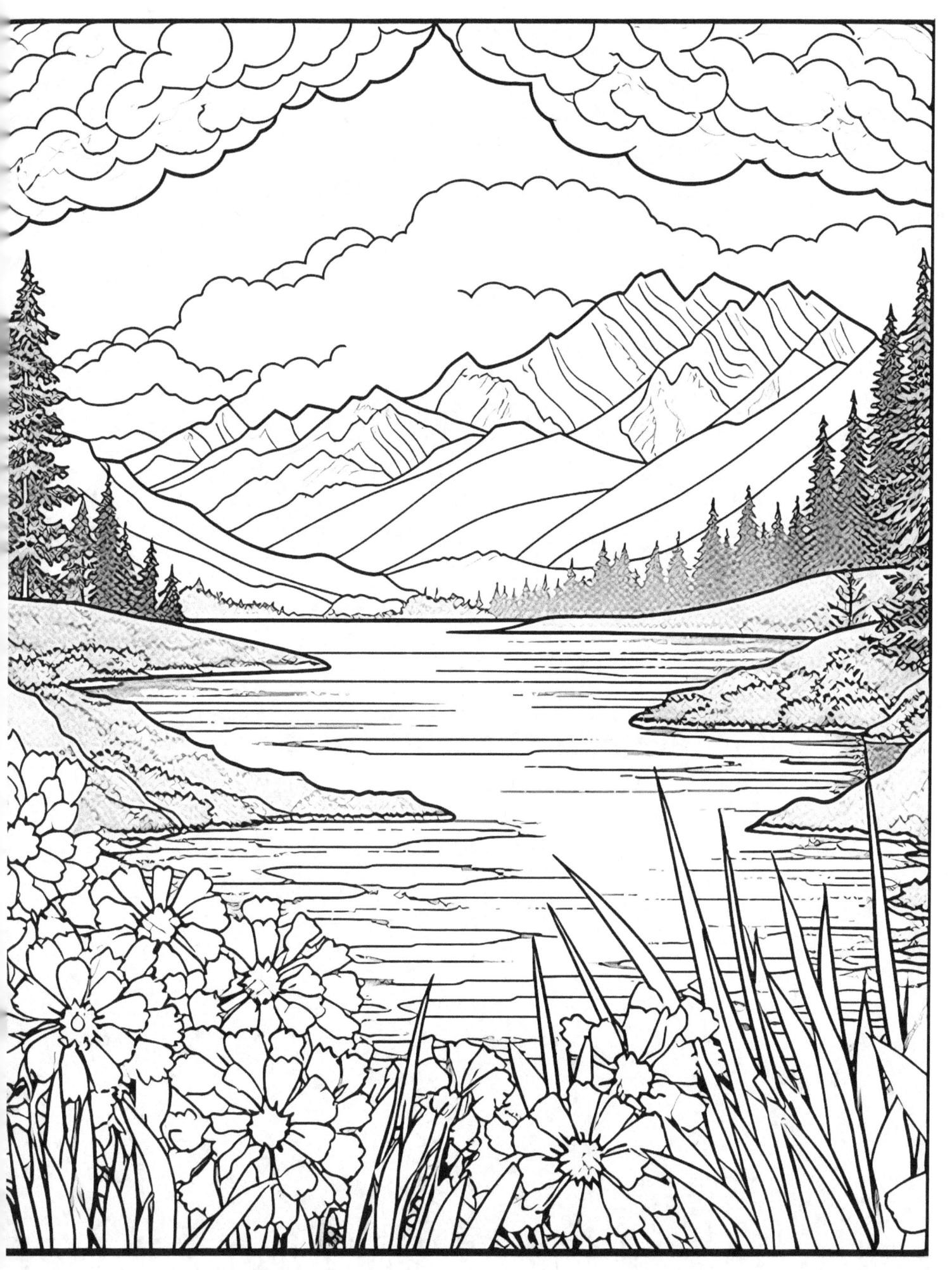

Whispers in the wind,

Storms dissolve in gentle breeze,

Guiding light unveiled.

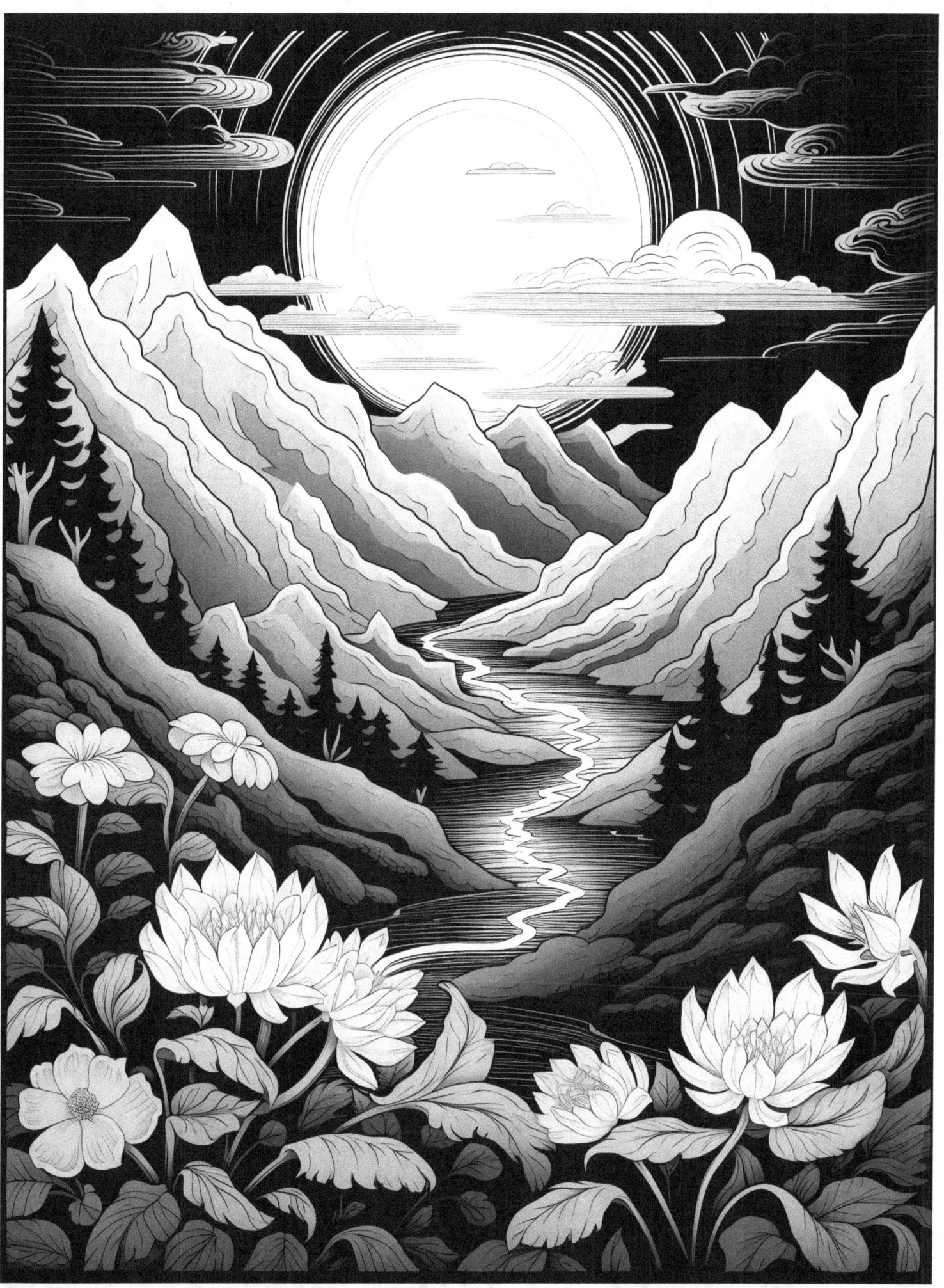

Nature's warm embrace,

Retreat in tranquil refuge,

Comfort found in green.

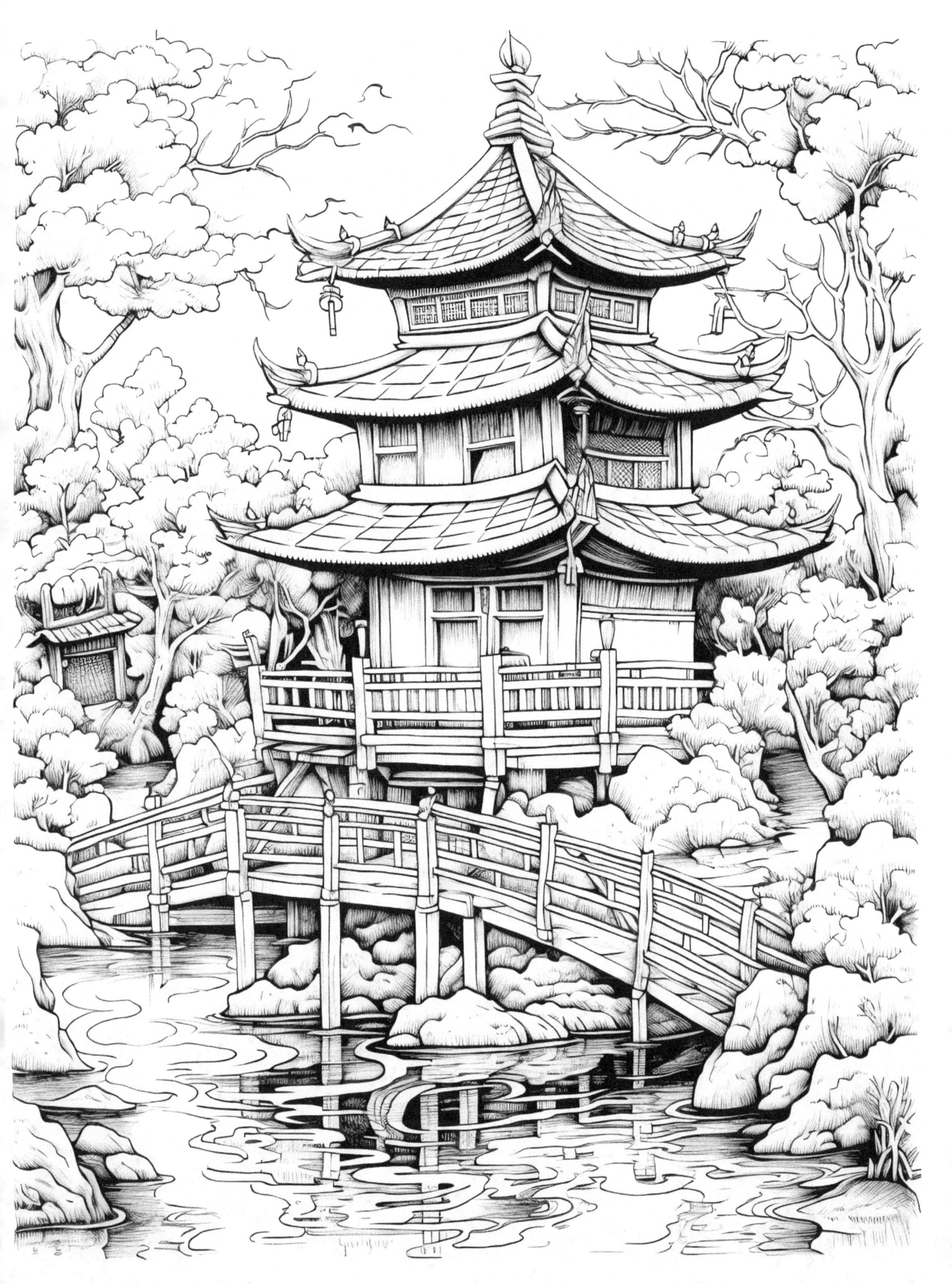

Footprints on new soil,

Exploring the unknown realms,

Courage maps the way.

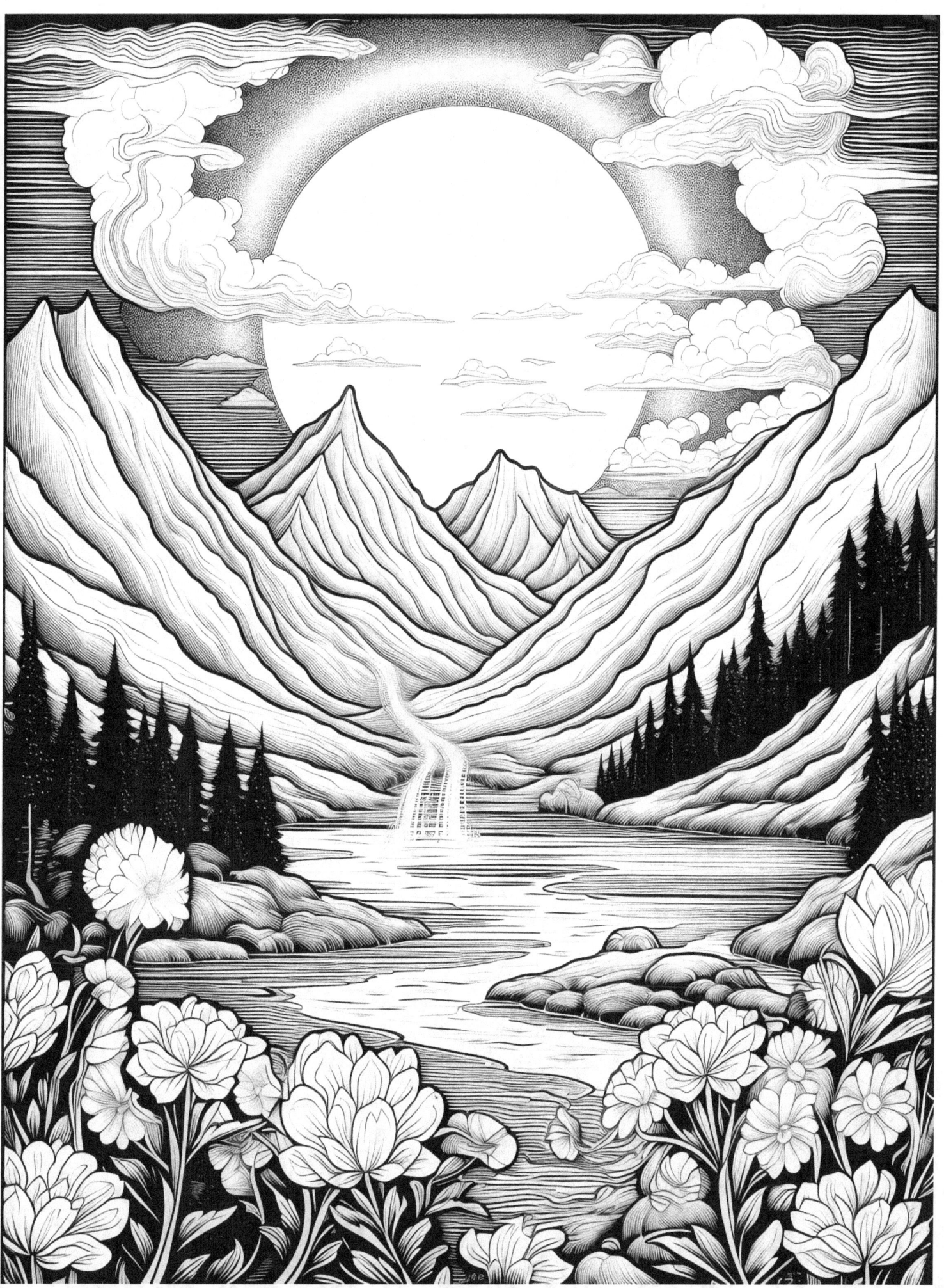

Chasing the sun's kiss,

New horizons beckon, dance,

Golden dreams take flight.

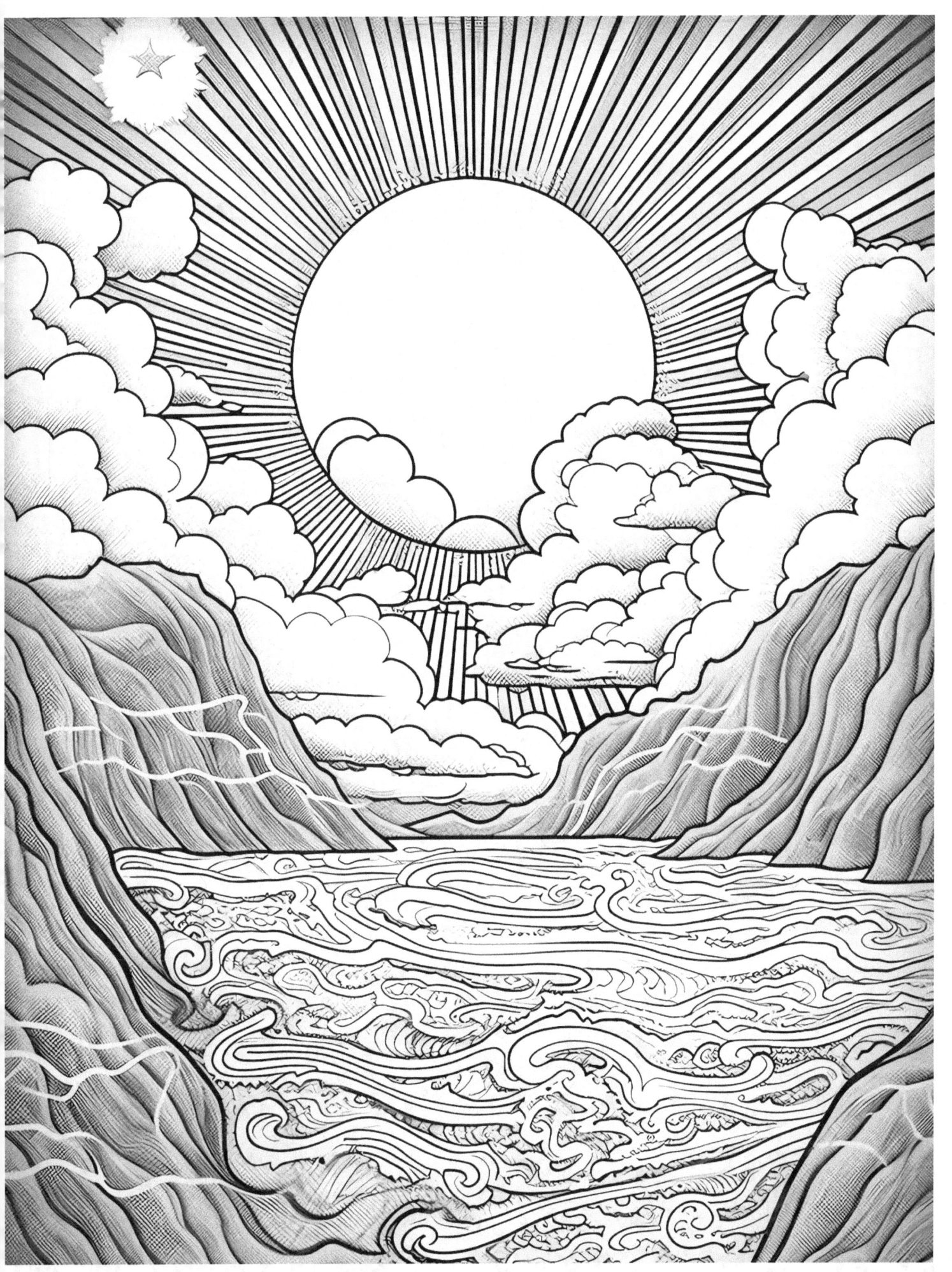